FACTS AT YOUR FINGERTIPS

THE WORLD OF ENDANGERED ANIMALS
SOUTH AND CENTRAL ASIA

BROWN BEAR BOOKS

J591.68
FAC

Published by Brown Bear Books Limited

4877 N. Circulo Bujia
Tucson, AZ 85718
USA

and

First Floor
9-17 St. Albans Place
London N1 ONX
UK

© 2014 Brown Bear Books Ltd

Library of Congress Cataloging-in-Publication Data available upon request.

ISBN-13 978-1-78121-077-2

In this book you will see the following key at top left of each entry. The key shows the level of threat faced by each animal, as judged by the International Union for the Conservation of Nature (IUCN).

EX	Extinct
EW	Extinct in the Wild
CR	Critically Endangered
EN	Endangered
VU	Vulnerable
NT	Near Threatened
LC	Least Concern
O	Other (this includes Data Deficient [DD] and Not Evaluated [NE])

For a few animals that have not been evaluated since 2001, the old status of Lower Risk still applies and this is shown by the letters **LR** on the key.

For more information on Categories of Threat, see pp. 54–57.

Editorial Director: Lindsey Lowe
Editor: Tim Harris
Design Manager: Keith Davis
Designer: Lynne Lennon
Children's Publisher: Anne O'Daly
Production Director: Alastair Gourlay

Printed in the United States of America

062014
AG/5534

CONTENTS

Habitats, Threats, and Conservation

South and Central Asia is a vast area of contrasts and extremes. It is divided by the world's highest mountain range, the Himalaya, with the highest peak of all—Mount Everest—rising to 29,035 feet (8,850 metres). To the north of the range, much of Central Asia is semi-arid grassland that is bitterly cold and inhospitable in winter but which has a surprising diversity of animal life for the rest of the year. There are also areas of desert, such as the vast Gobi Desert in Mongolia. In contrast, much of South Asia has a tropical monsoon climate so it is hot all year with heavy seasonal rains and a dry season. This climate supports forests and rich grasslands, although in many areas these environments have been cleared or cultivated.

Roof of the World

To the north of the Himalaya chain is the high Tibetan Plateau, for good reason sometimes called "the roof of the world." This has animals ranging from wild yak and wild ass to snow leopard and ground-feeding birds. The plateau is an unforgiving environment, especially in winter. Several of Asia's greatest rivers have their source there, including the Mekong, Salween, Ganges, Indus, Yangtze, and Yellow rivers.

Stretching from the plateau to the west and north are the huge expanses of the Central Asian grasslands (steppes) and semideserts. A few hundred Przewalski's wild horses—the only truly wild horses in the world—graze the steppes of Mongolia, and rapidly declining steppe pikas fight a losing battle against habitat change in their native Kazakhstan. Bordering that country is the world's largest lake, the Caspian Sea, which has an area four times greater than Lake Superior. Several thousand miles to the east, in southern Siberia, is Lake Baikal, which—at 5,371 feet (1,637 metres)—is the world's deepest lake. It is home for many unique plant and animal species, including tens of thousands of freshwater Baikal seals and many species of fish and aquatic invertebrates. Eighty percent of the lake's animal species are endemic, meaning they are found nowhere else.

The Himalaya

The highest peaks of the Himalaya range support few animals, but snow leopards can eke out an existence at almost 15,000 feet (4,500 metres), and markhors and takins also live on rocky mountain slopes. At lower altitudes, below the tree-line, there are lesser pandas and a varied selection of pheasants and other birds, including Temminck's tragopans. At the eastern end of the Himalaya, in southwest China, are giant pandas and black crested gibbons. Lower still, biodiversity increases further. In Chitwan National Park, Nepal, for example, a World Heritage Site, there are at least 42 species of mammal and more than 500 different birds have been recorded. The forest mammals at Chitwan include tiger, sloth bear, great Indian rhinoceros, Indian pangolin, rhesus monkey, and hanuman langur; clouded leopard has occurred but is not thought to be regular. Among the birds are wetland species, including kingfishers and the Vulnerable lesser adjutant stork, while the Critically Endangered Bengal florican lives on the grassland.

Western and Eastern Ghats

South of the Himalaya range is the relatively more gentle landscape of the Deccan Plateau of India. India is certainly not all flat. The relatively gentle mountain ranges of the Western Ghats and Eastern Ghats, because they have been harder to cultivate, still support important areas of forest and some animal species that are restricted to the mountains. The Western Ghats are a center of endemism: 84 species of amphibian, 16 birds, and seven mammals are found nowhere else in the world. Species that are protected in the mountains' national parks include tiger, gaur, sloth bear, Asian elephant, and Nilgiri tahr. One of the endemic birds is the Endangered black-chinned laughing-thrush. The Critically Endangered Jerdon's courser lives in thick vegetation in the Eastern Ghats though it is rarely seen.

Much of lowland India has been given over to cultivation, though a few forested areas still support very small populations of tigers, while Asian elephants are more widespread. Lowland wetlands attract millions of waterbirds from fall to spring, when they migrate

Climate change and the resultant increase in sea level could be a threat to many low-lying coastal regions around the Indian Ocean, such as Bangladesh and the Andaman Islands.

south from the bitterly cold winter weather farther north. The shallow, monsoon-flooded wetland of the Rann of Kutch, on the border of India and Pakistan, is one such example. When it fills with water it supports enormous numbers of ducks, herons, pelicans, and birds of prey. Nearby, in Gir Forest, is the world's last remaining population of Asiatic lions, numbering fewer than 500 of these magnificent predators.

Deserts and Coast

To the west again is the Arabian Peninsula, a region of vast deserts, where only the hardiest creatures can survive. These include the Endangered Arabian oryx and the Nubian ibex. The warm saline (salty) waters that encompass the Arabian Peninsula, from the Red Sea in the west to the Persian Gulf in the east, have many coral reefs, though these are threatened by coastal

The Amur Falcon Success Story

One particularly dramatic conservation success story took place in northeast India in 2013. More than 1 million Amur falcons use Doyand Reservoir, in Nagaland, as a stopover in fall on their way from eastern Siberia to East Africa. In fall 2012 it was discovered that hunters had used nets to trap up to 100,000 of these birds of prey as they roosted. The birds were then killed and smoked for sale as food. Amur falcon is not endangered at present, but if it suffers several years of trapping on this scale, it will be. The Indian partner of BirdLife International, the Bombay Natural History Society, worked with local people through schools and churches to explain how important their area was for the migrating falcons. "Friends of the Amur Falcon" groups were set up in schools to get the conservation message across to children. The strategy paid off in 2013 because not a single Amur falcon was trapped. Now the challenge is to keep the campaign going.

development, pollution, and a warming of the world's oceans as a result of climate change. Elsewhere—for example, around sections of the Bay of Bengal—mangrove forest borders the coast. In India, Sunderbans National Park, in the Ganges Delta, supports a population of tigers, and there are also river terrapins (Critically Endangered), South Asian river dolphins (Endangered), and olive ridley turtles (Vulnerable).

Pressure on the Land

Most of the threats faced by animals in the region arise from a growing human population. Sometimes these threats are direct—for example, with increased levels of hunting and fishing. Usually, however, they are indirect. More people need to be fed, so more land is given over to agriculture and this often—though it does not have to—means wetlands are drained, forests are cleared, and grasslands plowed. As the human population grows, so does the need for more homes, schools, hospitals, and roads, all of which have to be built somewhere. The animals that depend on reedbeds, mature forest, and open grassland lose areas in which to feed and raise their young and are concentrated into small areas. Animals that need large home ranges simply cannot be squeezed into smaller areas, so their population declines. Even if a forest is not cleared, if a road is driven into it, predators find it easier to get into the forest's heart, and mammals and birds that cannot cope with disturbance suffer.

In some parts of the region people's extreme poverty takes its toll on wildlife. People without electricity in their homes have to cut wood from forests to supply fuel for warmth and cooking. People without ready access to protein from any other source are compelled to hunt whatever animals they can. Until these issues are addressed there will always be a threat to wild animal populations. Hunting is one problem that is usually driven by extreme poverty. For example, fishers along the coasts of Bangladesh and Myanmar use nets to catch feeding shorebirds for food. They do not select which species to catch so Critically Endangered spoon-billed sandpipers are caught and killed alongside more common birds. Agencies such as BirdLife International have started to work with fishing communities to persuade people to stop this practice. As long as the people remain desperately poor, however, they could always return to bird-netting out of desperation.

Forest understory *is often removed by burning, as here, before the trees are felled to make way for agriculture or development.*

Asian Elephant

Elephas maximus

Asian elephants are valued as working animals so they will probably never become extinct. However, wild populations face serious threats.

The Asian elephant is smaller than the African elephant. Found across South and Southeast Asia, the Asian elephant has already died out in the eastern and western ends of its former range. There are a few hundred Asian elephants in the world's zoos, but few are bred in captivity.

Unlike their African cousins, Asian elephants have for centuries been trained and used as draft (working) animals. Today there are over 10,000 Asian elephants trained for heavy tasks. Ironically, they are used to help drag out felled trees from the forest, the environment on which wild Asian elephants depend.

Huge areas of forest have already been cut down, and losses continue all the time. With the destruction of the forests remnant elephant populations get split into smaller groups that become isolated from each other. In order to meet and breed, it is often necessary to cross developed land, with all the dangers that entails. In a project in Indonesia some elephants that became isolated in this way were actively driven out to join with others in a larger area of habitat.

Elephants need a lot of space: An individual's home range is often up to 15 square miles (40 sq. km) and sometimes over 116 square miles (300 sq. km) in southern India.

The animals need to drink over 11 gallons (50 liters) of water a day, so it is essential that they live near rivers or lakes—exactly the type of land that is considered ideal for agricultural use. Replacing the forests with farmland gives the elephants little choice but to raid the new crops such as bananas and sugarcane. As a result, farmers are inclined to shoot and snare the elephants.

A female Asian elephant *and her calf. Asian elephants live in small family groups of females and their young; most males (bulls) live in bachelor herds. There are about 27,000 elephants in India, but only about 1,500 of them are adult "tuskers" (animals with ivory tusks).*

Elephants need to eat at least 300 lb (150 kg) of plants every day. Such quantities are only available naturally in the lush tropical forests. Even in the fastest-growing forests the elephants need to move around in order to find sufficient food. The animals migrate seasonally between different feeding areas to overcome food shortages during the dry season. However, such movements are now prevented by roads

DATA PANEL

Asian elephant (Indian elephant)

Elephas maximus

Family: Elephantidae

World population: At least 41,000, plus several thousand captive animals

Distribution: India east to China, south to Vietnam and Indonesia; Sri Lanka

Habitat: Tropical forest and grasslands

Size: Length head/body: 18–21 ft (5.5–6.4 m); tail: 4–5 ft (1.2–1.5 m); height at shoulder: 8.2–10 ft (2.5–3 m). Weight: females up to 6,000 lb (2,720 kg); males up to 12,000 lb (5,400 kg)

Form: Huge animal with long trunk; columnlike legs. Differs from African elephant in having a rounded back, smaller ears, and domed head. Tusks often absent, especially in females

Diet: Leaves, grass, and bark; also soil to obtain minerals

Breeding: Single calf born at any time of year after gestation period of about 22 months. Life span up to 80 years

Related endangered species: African elephant *(Loxodonta africana)* VU

Status: IUCN EN

and farmland. Even national parks may not be large enough to accommodate populations of elephants all year round, so special dispersal "corridors" have been created to link areas of forest and enable elephants to migrate seasonally between them. (The Kallar Jaccanari corridor, for example, links the 4,000 elephants of the northern and southern Nilghiri Biosphere Reserve in southern India.) The corridors have to be about 8 miles (13 km) wide.

Wasteful Killing

Shooting and snaring for ivory have been a threat to the Asian elephant for centuries, although the females do not have tusks, and the males sometimes lack

them. (The African elephant has always been under greater threat from hunting for tusks.) Trading in ivory is now forbidden under the CITES agreement.

Another threat to the Asian elephant is the millions of land mines left in the forests of Sri Lanka, Cambodia, Vietnam, and other Asian countries during wars in the 20th century. In Sri Lanka it is estimated that each year about 20 elephants die after stepping on land mines. Others are crippled.

Steppe Pika

Ochotona pusilla

The decline of the steppe pika is a long-term trend dating back to the early days of agriculture. The main cause of the decline is habitat loss.

Pikas are short-eared cousins of rabbits and hares, and in some parts of the world they can be exceedingly common. They are well suited to life in a harsh climate; their short legs, small, rounded ears, thick fur, and furry feet are all adaptations to the cold weather. They can survive long winters under deep snow, where they remain active in networks of hidden tunnels in moist soil.

Being snowbound for several months obviously restricts the pikas' foraging options, so over the summer they spend much of their time preparing for the winter by collecting as much extra food as possible. Grass and leaves are harvested, allowed to dry in the sun, and gathered together in haystacks. A single pika can gather several pounds of winter fodder in one stack; and while this in itself is not enough to support the animal through the winter, it provides an essential supplement to the meager winter rations.

Decline in Numbers

Over two-thirds of the world's 26 pika species are currently threatened with extinction in the wild. One of the most notable declines has been that of the Russian steppe pika, in spite of the fact that pika populations have a quite extraordinary capacity for growth under the right conditions. A single female steppe pika can easily produce five litters of 10 babies each in a season. Assuming that half of them are females (that mature within one month and soon begin to breed themselves), by the onset of winter the family could include over 1,000 animals, every one a child or grandchild of the original female. In a good season even the first-born grandchildren may breed, in which case the potential for growth reaches staggering proportions.

However, pika populations can disappear even faster than they build up. Populations of the Russian steppe pika vary between 0.04 and 33 animals per acre (0.1 and 80 animals per ha). These wild fluctuations are perfectly natural, and in a stable environment there are usually enough survivors of a crash to reestablish the population. Cycles of boom and bust restrict the genetic

DATA PANEL

Steppe pika

Ochotona pusilla

Family: Ochotonidae

World population: Unknown, but declining rapidly

Distribution: Steppes of Russia and Kazakhstan, between Volga and Irtysh rivers

Habitat: Open plains, deserts, and dry grasslands

Size: Length: 5–12 in (12.5–30 cm). Weight: 4.5–14 oz (125–400 g)

Form: Dumpy, grayish-brown animal resembling small, round-eared rabbit with no visible tail and short legs; thick, dense fur

Diet: Plant material, including leaves of grasses, sedges, and herbs; also twigs and flowers of woody plants

Breeding: Between 3 and 5 litters of 3–13 young born throughout spring and summer, after gestation period of about 1 month; young mature at 1 month. Life span more than 5 years in the wild

Related endangered species: Helan Shan pika *(Ochotona helanshanensis)* CR; Koslov's pika *(O. koslowi)* EN

Status: IUCN LC

Pikas, *also sometimes called mouse hares, are small, rabbitlike creatures that are found in parts of western North America, Asia, and eastern Europe. The steppe pika (right) lives in the steppes of Russia and Kazakhstan.*

variability of a population, however, and the problem becomes especially acute when pika populations are isolated by farmland or other human developments. Reduced variability makes small, postcrash populations even more vulnerable to local catastrophes, be they natural (fire, drought, disease, or hard winters) or persecution by humans (especially by poisoning). Pikas need grass and other vegetation to support their large numbers, but it is destroyed along with their burrows when land is plowed. As farmland increasingly dominates the landscape, the pikas lose out.

Crop Raiders

Changes in land use during the Middle Ages drove the steppe pikas out of large parts of their former range in what is now the Ukraine. The western part of the pika's range continued to be eroded in the following centuries, and by the early 19th century there were no pikas west of the Volga River. The remaining populations are fragmented and at risk of being poisoned, snared, or shot. Their habitat is disappearing under farmland, leaving the pikas little choice but to raid crops, provoking the hatred of farmers and plantation owners. The tender saplings of newly planted conifer plantations make easy pickings during the winter, when the trees are buried in the snow and the pikas can feed without being seen. The extent of their attacks on the trees becomes all too evident when the snow melts, but then it is too late to act, and the trees die. The frustration of landowners on finding their crops nibbled and ruined after the spring thaw is understandable. As long as humans and pikas compete for a living on the steppes, the future of this hardy and naturally prolific little animal is at risk.

Black Crested Gibbon

Nomascus concolor

Black crested gibbons are distinctive and social creatures that bring benefits to their forest habitats. If they are allowed to become extinct, there could be severe consequences for an entire ecosystem.

There are nine species of gibbon in South and Southeast Asia, all of which look fairly similar and have a similar way of life. They spend most of their time high in the forest canopy, where they feed on leaves and fruit. They have amazingly long, strong arms, powerful shoulders, and hook-shaped hands, which enable them to swing from branch to branch or simply dangle for hours at a time.

Most gibbon species are monogamous, which means that a single male and female form a bond that lasts until one of them dies. Black crested gibbons, however, are polygynous: A single male black crested gibbon may have a harem of up to four females, and they all live with their offspring of various ages.

Gibbons are famed for their haunting songs and loud hooting calls; they produce whooping sounds that carry for huge distances through the forest. The sounds are usually performed by a bonded pair, but often the whole family joins in. Other important group activities include grooming and play—the youngsters are full of fun, and sometimes the whole group participates in their antics. The gibbons seem to delight in their acrobatic skill, and no one watching them could fail to be entertained. This means, however, that many baby gibbons are taken from the wild to be kept as pets.

Young gibbons normally stay with their mothers for several years, only leaving to seek mates of their own when they are seven or eight years old. Without their mother they cannot learn many of the skills they need to survive in the wild. In captivity most end up serving a lonely and miserable life sentence and develop abnormally limited behavior patterns.

Illegal Hunting

Most of the black crested gibbons' problems are, in fact, relatively recent. They do not suffer unduly from predation and have lived harmoniously with humans for many thousands of years. It seems that early forest people respected the gibbons and left them in peace; hunting (by humans) is a recent threat.

In China black crested gibbons are legally protected, and many live in reserves. However, people break the law to obtain black crested gibbon meat, which is considered a delicacy; gibbon bones also fetch a good price for use in eastern medicines that are supposed to help relieve rheumatism. The booming

DATA PANEL

Black crested gibbon

Nomascus concolor

Family: Hylobatidae

World population: 1,300–2,000 (2006 estimate), declining

Distribution: Vietnam, Laos, and Yunnan province, southern China

Habitat: Closed canopy evergreen forests

Size: Height: 18–25 in (46–68 cm); males and females similar size. Weight: 11–17 lb (5–8 kg)

Form: Slender ape with long arms and hook-shaped hands; fur dense and silky. Mature males black with white cheeks; breeding females pale buff

Diet: Ripe fruit, tender young leaves, and buds, some invertebrates

Breeding: Single young born every 2–3 years after gestation of 7–8 months; weaned at about 2 years; mature at about 8 years. Life span up to 25 years

Related endangered species: Silvery Javan gibbon (*Hylobates moloch*) EN; other gibbons also face similar threats

Status: IUCN CR

Chinese economy is making more money available for purchasing these products, regardless of the law, and illegal hunting is undoubtedly a growing problem. The main cause of the black crested gibbon's decline, however, is another all too familiar one: Local human populations have increased by about 50 percent in less than 25 years. The resulting expansion of human communities into the gibbons' habitat has caused a disastrous drop in gibbon numbers.

Added Value

Black crested gibbons eat mostly fruit, and in doing so they provide a valuable service to the forest trees. Most fruits have seeds that will pass through a gibbon's digestive system unharmed; in fact, some appear not to germinate unless they have been eaten and then deposited in the gibbon's dung. In the few million years since gibbons first appeared in the region, the trees of South and Southeast Asia have evolved to bear fruit at different times of the year. Consequently, there is always a good chance of the fruit being eaten and the seeds dispersed far and wide, along with a helping of manure fertilizer, which gets the seedling off to a good start. To allow the black crested gibbon to become extinct would not only be a tragic loss to humankind, but also their disappearance could have drastic consequences for an entire ecosystem.

On a note of optimism, however, it seems that the gibbons can return to areas of previously felled forest that have been allowed to regenerate. With careful management and goodwill it should be possible to restore black crested gibbon populations to at least some of the areas from which they have disappeared.

The black crested gibbon *probably evolved as a separate species about 1 million years ago. It differs from other gibbons in its coat markings and social behavior. Mature males (right) are black with buff cheeks, while breeding females (left) are pale buff.*

Russian Desman

Desmana moschata

The Russian desman—an amphibious relative of the mole—has been hunted extensively for its fur. It has also suffered as a result of water pollution and from competition with introduced species.

Desmans were once widespread across Europe, and fossils have been found as far west as Britain. However, only two species now exist: one that is found in the Pyrenees mountains of northern Spain and southwestern France, and the other in Kazakhstan, Russia, and the Ukraine. Both species are classified as Vulnerable. The Pyrenean desman and the Russian desman both have populations numbering in the low thousands—and both are getting even more scarce.

Little is known about the basic biology and social organization of the desman. It is an amphibious mammal that gets more than half of its food from hunting in water. The Pyrenean desman seems to be a solitary creature with a small, permanent home range. It prefers cool lakes and fast-flowing rivers. In places it lives at altitudes of more than 5,500 feet (1,800 m).

Unlike the Pyrenean desman, the Russian desman appears to be nomadic, although it has been recorded living in shared burrows. Its preferred habitat is lakes and slow-flowing water. Desmans build their burrows among the waterside vegetation in which they hunt for food, but they also use the water plants as camouflage to hide from predators.

Hunted to Extinction

Like mink and muskrats, desmans have a coat that has dense, soft underfur and long, glossy "guard" hairs. This two-layer coat effectively insulates the animals against rapid heat loss in the cold water. Unfortunately for the animals, it also provides a superb fur for fashionable garments. Russian desman numbers were severely affected by hunting during the 19th century because of the value of the silky coat. Hundreds of thousands of desmans were killed for the fur trade: In just two years over 300,000 skins were sold to China, and at the beginning of the 20th century about 20,000 skins were being processed each year.

Since desmans rarely travel far from water, traps set along river banks and lake shores were an effective method of capture. If trapping persisted for any length of time, the entire population could be wiped out locally. Fishermen setting nets to catch small fish

DATA PANEL

Russian desman

Desmana moschata

Family: Talpidae

World population: Fewer than 30,000, declining

Distribution: Kazakhstan; river systems of the Don, Ural, and Volga in southwestern Russia; the Ukraine

Habitat: Permanently wet habitats, river edges, lakes, and marshes

Size: Length head/body: 7–9 in (18–22 cm); tail: 7–8.5 in (17–21.5 cm). Weight: 1.75–3.5 oz (50–100 g)

Form: Ratlike mammal with long, flexible nose and long, glossy hair. Tail scaly and flattened from side to side; partially webbed feet. Various parts of body have sensory whiskers

Diet: Aquatic insects, mollusks, fish, and frogs

Breeding: Families of 3–5 young produced twice per year. Life span unknown, probably 2–3 years

Related endangered species: Pyrenean desman (*Galemys pyrenaicus*) VU

Status: IUCN VU

often captured desmans as well and may sometimes have done so deliberately. The desmans represented a valuable addition to the normal catch.

Once the Russian desman had been officially recognized as rare in 1929, it was given legal protection and most trapping ended. However, other threats loomed. Hydroelectric projects affected water flow and therefore the suitability of the habitat for both the desman and its diet of aquatic invertebrates. Habitat disturbance forced desmans to move on, seeking new places in which to live and feed. In addition, grazing farm animals and riverside development removed the vegetation from long stretches of bank, taking away the desman's refuges and leading to their local extinction.

A further threat has come from introduced rodents such as the muskrat (from North America) and the coypu (from South America). Kept on fur farms, they were released or escaped into the desman's home

waters. They have competed for burrows and shelter, eaten waterside plants, and successfully displaced the smaller desman.

Water quality has been affected by industrial and agricultural pollution. The influx of nutrients—particularly as a result of fertilizer runoff from farmland—encourages the growth of algae. The algae multiply, using all the oxygen and turning the water into a dense green "soup." The lack of oxygen also kills insects and crustaceans, the main food of desmans.

Recently, conservationists have captured more than 10,000 Russian desmans and released them into places where competition and pollution threats are less serious. The animals have also been reintroduced to parts of their range where they had become extinct. Reintroduction works only where the original threat (hunting) is being controlled, and where the habitat remains suitable. There are now special refuges set aside to protect surviving desman populations, but numbers continue to decline.

Conservationists have recommended other measures to help the desmans, including banning the unrestricted sale of nets and net-making materials and developing a system of measures to combat the use of electric landing nets.

The desman *is adapted for foraging in water. It has partially webbed feet and extrasensitive whiskers on the muzzle. It also has hypersensitive hairs on its tail and legs, and its nostrils and ears can be closed by valves.*

Baikal Seal

Pusa sibirica

The icy waters of Siberia's Lake Baikal are a challenging place to live at the best of times. The added problems of disease, pollution, and a long-established sealing industry are putting the Baikal seal under considerable pressure.

Lake Baikal in Siberia is the deepest and oldest lake in the world. It is home to many remarkable plants and animals, including the only species of seal that spends its entire life in and around fresh water: the Baikal seal.

There is a long history of seal hunting on Lake Baikal, with pelts, meat, and oil providing an important contribution to the local economy. In the 1930s overhunting was seriously threatening the Baikal seals, and a system of quotas was introduced, allowing only limited numbers to be hunted each year. The population recovered steadily, and concern for the species subsided. However, in recent years the seals' fortunes appear to have taken a turn for the worse. Between 1994 and 2000 the population declined by as much as 20 percent. There are several interrelated reasons for this alarming development.

Victims of the Hunt

In the late 1990s seal-hunting quotas stood at about 6,000 seals per year. However, the figure did not include the many seals that were killed or injured in the hunt but not removed from the water. Some reports suggest that for every seal landed, a further three died but sank before they could be retrieved. Official statistics for the period 2004–2006 reported about 2,000 seals had been killed annually, but it was also estimated that there had been 1,500–4,000 "uncounted" deaths each year, mostly casualties of fishing bycatch and poaching. Since most hunting happens in the northern parts of the lake, the seals prefer to breed farther south. However, temperatures in the south are warmer than those in the north, and the snow lairs in which the young are born melt earlier, leaving the pups exposed to bad weather and predators, including brown bears and large crows.

To add to the seal's difficulties, the waters in which they feed are highly polluted. Chemicals from industry—as well as pesticides, including the notorious DDT—pour into the lake and accumulate in the bodies of invertebrates, fish, and seals. Mother seals inevitably pass on large doses of pollutants to their young, both in the womb and through their milk. There is no

RUSSIA — Lake Baikal — MONGOLIA — CHINA

DATA PANEL

Baikal seal (nerpa)

Pusa sibirica

Family: Phocidae

World population: More than 80,000

Distribution: Lake Baikal, Russia

Habitat: Fresh water

Size: Length: 3.6–4.6 ft (1–1.4 m). Weight: 110–286 lb (50–130 kg)

Form: Small seal with relatively large front flippers; fur is dark gray-brown on back, paler beneath; pups have creamy-white coats

Diet: Freshwater fish; invertebrates

Breeding: Single young (sometimes twins), born February–March after 9-month gestation; weaned at 8.5–11 weeks; females mature at 6 years, males at 7 years. May live up to 56 years

Related endangered species: Baltic gray seal (*Halichooerus grypus*) EN; Mediterranean monk seal (*Monachus monachus*) CR; Hawaiian monk seal (*M. schauinslandi*) CR; Caspian seal (*Phoca caspica*) EN

Status: IUCN LC

doubt that pollution is at least partly responsible for a doubling of the infant death rate in recent years. The effects on older seals include failure to breed and weakened immunity to disease. In 1988 some 5,000 Baikal seals died from a form of distemper virus, and in the late 1990s there were hundreds of unexplained seal deaths suspiciously close to industrial sites along the lake shore.

Crisis Point

Lake Baikal has been made a World Heritage Site and includes several nature reserves and national parks. In theory the Baikal seals should also be protected, but in practice little is done. Indeed, one national park was so short of money that wardens were asked to help raise funds by leading trophy hunters on expeditions to shoot seals. The majority of seals that die each year are young. As a result, the main population consists of elderly animals; while older seals die or become infertile, fewer young healthy ones are starting to breed. The scale of the crisis for the Baikal seal is only just being realized. The health of the population is now being monitored closely, but tackling the varied causes of the seals' decline will be costly and difficult.

Baikal seals *are descendants of seals that arrived sometime during the last ice age, when Lake Baikal was connected to the Arctic Ocean. Ice is still a factor in the lake. In May and June, after they have bred, many adult seals migrate to the colder north of the lake so that they can molt relatively undisturbed on areas of ice.*

Sloth Bear

Melursus ursinus

Sloth bears are peaceful creatures that are sensitive to disturbance. Excessively hunted in the past, they are now scarce and have gained legal protection in some areas.

Sloth bears are so named because they were once thought to be a kind of Indian sloth. The mistake is understandable, since the first specimens were known only from skins brought to the British Museum in London in the late 18th century.

Bear-Faced

The sloth bear's face sets it apart from other bears. It has a long, hairless snout and no front teeth. Its lips are soft and able to form a tube that is pushed out to suck up food. The roof of the mouth has a large hollow to facilitate huge suction. The bear is also able to close its nostrils to keep insects from crawling inside its snout and to prevent its nose from filling with soil when rooting around for food. Termites form the main part of the bear's diet. The sloth bear uses its

3-inch- (7.6-cm-) long front claws to break into termite mounds, then pushes its snout into the hole and sucks up termites, eggs, and grubs.

The sloth bear is a true omnivore and will eat just about anything. It is partial to sweet, energy-rich foods, and its long claws are effective at breaking up bees' nests to get at the honey. Fruit is a favorite food, and the bear can climb well to reach it. Some bears will shake trees to dislodge ripe fruit. They also eat crops such as sugarcane, corn, and yams, and will devour any meat they find, although they do not appear to catch and kill their own prey. Feeding occurs at night, but the bears will come out at any time of day.

Adult sloth bears mate during June and July (except in Sri Lanka, where they appear to mate all year round). Mating is preceded by a boisterous courtship involving play-fights and plenty of bear-hugs! Females are pregnant for six or seven months. The embryos that they carry probably spend the first weeks in a state of suspended

DATA PANEL

Sloth bear

Melursus ursinus

Family: Ursidae

World population: 10,000–25,000

Distribution: Possibly Bangladesh, Bhutan, India, Nepal, and Sri Lanka

Habitat: Forests

Size: Length: 4.6–6.2 ft (1.4–1.9 m); height at shoulder: 23–35 in (60–90 cm); male larger than female. Weight: 198–286 lb (90–135 kg)

Form: A shaggy black bear with a u-shaped band of creamy-white fur on its chest. It has distinctive long, tubular lips that are used to suck up small items of food

Diet: Termites, fruit, honey, crops, including sugarcane and corn, eggs, carrion, and sometimes flowers

Breeding: Between 1 and 3 cubs (usually 2) born December–January. Lives up to 30 years in captivity

Related endangered species: Spectacled bear (*Tremarctos ornatus*) VU

Status: IUCN VU

animation, resuming development later in the year. The young are born in the middle of the dry season when conditions are favorable.

Threats

The peaceful sloth bear faces many dangers. For years young sloth bears were taken into captivity after their mothers were killed and trained to perform tricks. A less obvious but more dangerous threat comes from the creation of huge plantations that replace the varied natural forest. The plantations tend to cultivate single species of tree, so forests remain but no longer offer enough food variety to support the bears.

Sloth bears are rather shy animals and do not adjust well to disturbance. The felling of trees, expansion of farmland, and construction of roads and dams all intrude into the bears' forest home and drive

Sloth bears have no reason to hibernate, since there is plenty of food all year round. However, they do build dens in which to care for their young.

them away. Increasingly, there is nowhere else to go, and the sloth bear is now scarce. Their liking for crops makes them unpopular with farmers, so they are often trapped or hunted. The sloth bear's gall bladder is used in traditional medicines and fetches a high price, encouraging still more killing. The sale of sloth bear products is banned in parts of the species' range, and they are legally protected in some regions, but the law is difficult to enforce in remote areas. It is not known how well they will respond to conservation measures, nor even what can be done to assist them, other than to prevent hunting.

Lesser Panda

Ailurus fulgens

For about 50 years the lesser, or red, panda was the only known species of panda. Now the animal is experiencing many of the same problems as its more famous relative, the giant panda.

EX
EW
CR
EN
VU
NT
LC
O

The lesser, or red, panda lives in Himalayan forests at altitudes of between 6,500 and 15,750 feet (2,000 and 4,800 m). Slightly bigger than a domestic cat, it has thick, reddish-brown fur on most of its body, while the long tail is marked with conspicuous red and beige bands. Lesser pandas are excellent climbers, capable of scampering up and down trees headfirst. The tail is not prehensile (adapted for seizing or grasping), but nevertheless it makes an effective counterbalance. Lesser pandas have a waddling gait when moving on the ground due to the fact that their front legs are angled inward.

Like the giant panda, the lesser panda has an unusual thumb. In its ancestors the thumb was reduced to a mere claw, but when the animal began to adapt to a vegetarian diet, the ability to grip foliage became an advantage. Instead of replacing the thumb, however, natural selection favored a different arrangement—a small bone in the panda's wrist, called the radial sesamoid, enlarged to provide a substitute structure that the panda now uses to grasp food.

Although the panda is almost entirely herbivorous, its digestive system resembles that of a carnivore, with a simple stomach and a short gut. Most herbivores have long intestines to provide the digestive efficiency necessary to cope with their tough, fibrous food. The lesser panda's gut is not well adapted to a diet of plant material, so much of the nutritional value of the food it consumes is wasted. Pandas therefore have to eat more than other herbivores of similar size, and their metabolism is generally sluggish to help conserve energy. Unlike giant pandas, however, lesser pandas are not restricted to a bamboo diet; they also eat the leaves, flowers, fruit, roots, and bark of other plants,

and have been known to eat fungi and even insects, birds' eggs, and occasionally nestlings.

Lesser pandas mate early in the winter, and the young are born about 19 weeks later. Heavily pregnant females prepare for the births by furnishing a secure nest site, often in a tree hole or rocky crevice, with twigs, leaves, and grass. Here they have litters of between one and four cubs, which they tend more or less continuously for about a week. After that the mother spends increasingly long periods out of the nest foraging, but she returns regularly to suckle and clean her family, whom she recognizes individually by smell. This pattern continues for about three months until the young cubs are ready to leave the nest. To begin with, they do so only under the cover of darkness, and they stay very close to their mother.

The family will stay together for a short while longer, until the breeding season comes around again, and the mother drives the youngsters away. They then take up solitary lives and have little contact with other pandas. When two animals do meet, they may engage in a variety of raccoonlike displays, including back-arching, head-shaking, jaw-snapping, and standing up on two legs. If they survive to adulthood, the young pandas will be ready to breed themselves the following year, at about 18 months of age.

Puzzles and Problems

For years, zoologists debated whether the lesser panda belongs in the bear family (Ursidae) or with the raccoons (Procyonidae). Most now believe it should be in a family of its own—the Ailuridae.

While questions of classification puzzle zoologists, the lesser panda is facing several serious problems.

DATA PANEL

Lesser panda (red panda)

Ailurus fulgens

Family: Ursidae (sometimes placed in the raccoon family Procyonidae, or assigned its own family, the Ailuridae)

World population: Fewer than 10,000 mature animals

Distribution: Himalayan regions of Nepal, Bhutan, Myanmar (Burma), India, and China (Sichuan and Yunnan provinces)

Habitat: Forest at altitudes of 6,500–15,750 ft (2,000–4,800 m)

Size: Length head/body: 19–23 in (50–60 cm); tail: 12–20 in (30–51 cm). Weight: 6–13 lb (3–6 kg)

Form: Tree-dwelling, racoonlike animal, the size of a large domestic cat. Rich, chestnut-colored fur, darker on belly; tail is banded chestnut and beige; face attractively marked in beige and white

Diet: Berries, blossoms, birds' eggs, leaves of various plants, especially bamboo; also roots, vegetables, fruit, small birds, and mammals

Breeding: Between 1 and 4 young born in spring and summer (births peak in June). Life span probably 8–10 years, maximum 14

Related endangered species: Giant panda (*Ailuropoda melanoleuca*) EN

Status: IUCN VU

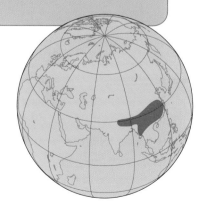

Deforestation and competition for space and resources from ever-increasing human populations are threatening the animal throughout its range. Commercial logging, the demand for firewood, slash-and-burn cultivation, and grazing domestic animals on previously forested areas are all problems. Pandas are also caught in traps intended for musk deer and are sometimes the victims of armed conflicts.

Lesser pandas
sometimes venture to the ground, but they are generally nocturnal and arboreal, spending most of the day sleeping in the trees and feeding there by night.

Dhole

Cuon alpinus

Centuries of intensive persecution and habitat destruction on a massive scale have taken their toll on this unusual wild dog, whose fascinating daily life has only recently been studied.

The highly adaptable dhole was once relatively common throughout a vast range that covered much of southern Russia, Mongolia, China, India, and Southeast Asia to Java. Like many other wild canids (members of the dog family), the dhole has suffered from severe prejudice.

Until quite recently the dhole could be killed with impunity throughout its range. To be fair, the species' dreadful reputation did have some basis in fact. Anyone who has witnessed a dhole kill could be forgiven for concluding that they are indeed wanton and unnecessarily cruel killers. Unlike most predators, which dispatch their prey with a fatal bite to the throat or spinal cord, dholes kill by ripping open the victim's belly, often beginning to eat well before the animal has bled to death. If such a kill is disturbed by people watching, the dholes retreat, and the victim may take even longer to die. It is easy enough to understand why a farmer or tribesman coming across such a scene of carnage—especially if it involved one of their own cattle or goats—would want to eliminate the dhole from the neighborhood.

Doting Dads

There is, however, another side to the dhole's nature. Like the painted hunting dog of Africa or the Amazonian bush dog, the dhole lives and hunts in packs that are models of cooperation and tolerance.

Within a pack the majority of individuals are male. Only one female in the group will breed, and the rest of the pack make it their business to protect and serve her family. When the pups are very young, the pack restricts its range to the region of the den, often leaving one of its number to stand guard over the precious family. The pack visits regularly, bringing food for the mother and her offspring. The pups will start eating regurgitated meat from the age of about three weeks. Later, when the youngsters are old enough to begin following the pack on hunting excursions, their doting relatives not only keep a close eye on them to ensure their safety, but they will also allow them first access to any kill. Dholes tend not to fight over food— each dog ensures its fair share by simply eating as fast as it can—and the pack hierarchy means that there is rarely any dispute over the right to mate.

Misunderstood

All in all, dholes are fascinating and misunderstood animals for whom the tide of opinion has just begun to turn. Even so, it is unlikely that the dhole will ever be popular with local people. There is no escaping the fact that they can and do kill livestock and game, and will continue to do so.

Past generations of dholes have been shot, snared, and poisoned. Now that the species is protected, such killings are illegal, but there is little doubt that they still take place. The greatest concern at present is over the status of two of the three Indian subspecies of dhole; the Himalayan and trans-Himalayan dholes are both thought to be on the verge of extinction. Numbers of the third Indian subspecies—the peninsular dhole— have rallied a little. Their small recovery is thanks largely to the establishment of nature reserves and national parks intended primarily to protect the tiger. Elsewhere in their range, dholes are surviving in ever-smaller fragments of habitat, often in very poor and remote areas where it is difficult for the authorities to enforce any ban on hunting.

DATA PANEL

Dhole (Asian wild dog)

Cuon alpinus

Family: Canidae

World population: Unknown

Distribution: Western Asia to China, India, and Malay Peninsula; Sumatra and Java

Habitat: Forest, wooded hill, and steppe; often rests in clearings but rarely seen in very large open spaces

Size: Length: up to 36 in (92 cm); height at shoulder: up to 20 in (50 cm). Weight: 37–44 lb (17–20 kg)

Form: Robust, collie-sized dog with light grayish-brown to rich-red coat and dark bushy tail; muzzle short and powerful; one fewer molar teeth than other canids

Diet: Insects, reptiles, and other mammals of any size up to large stag; occasionally berries and other fruit

Breeding: Litters of about 8 pups born November–March after 9-week gestation; mature after 1 year. Typical longevity unknown

Related endangered species: Red wolf (*Canis rufus*) CR; Ethiopian wolf (*C. simensis*) EN; African wild dog (*Lycaon pictus*) EN

Status: IUCN EN

The dhole
*is a seemingly
brutal killer but
also a cooperative
family carer.*

Snow Leopard

Panthera uncia

Superbly equipped for living on steep, rocky mountainsides that are blanketed with snow for much of the year, the snow leopard has evolved to cope with some of Asia's most hostile habitats. However, it is now becoming increasingly rare.

Generally classified alongside big cats of the genus *Panthera*, the snow leopard also shares some characteristics with small cats (genus *Felis*). For example, the structure of its voice box prevents it from producing the bloodcurdling roar of a big cat, and when feeding, a snow leopard adopts the crouching posture typical of a small cat.

The snow leopard's most striking features are undoubtedly its very deep fur, its long, thick, furry tail, and its big feet. All three are adaptations to living in cold and snowy conditions. The snow leopard has to contend with extremes of climate, and the thickness of the coat varies with the time of year. In winter it is up to 3 inches (8 cm) deep on the belly, but in summer it molts and becomes much finer. The long tail is also heavily furred, and the leopard uses it to cover the more exposed parts of its body when at rest. A sleeping snow leopard curls up with its tail wrapped over its nose and mouth to keep its breath from freezing. The snow leopard has relatively large feet, but the size is exaggerated by a thick covering of fur on each paw, even on the pads. The extra fur insulates the paws against the cold ground and helps spread the leopard's weight over a larger area, allowing it to walk over snow without sinking.

Typical snow leopard habitat is steep and rocky, with dry scrub or grassland vegetation that is covered with snow for most of the winter. Prey density is usually low, so the snow leopard travels over large distances to find food, moving to different altitudes with migrating prey such as wild sheep, ibex, and musk deer. The animal's lifestyle is generally solitary, though

DATA PANEL

Snow leopard

Panthera uncia

Family: Felidae

World population: 4,000–6,500 (2003 estimate), declining

Distribution: Found in widely scattered areas in the mountains of Central Asia, from northwestern China to the Himalaya; China probably supports more than half the world's population

Habitat: Steep, rocky mountains up to 14,760 feet (4,500 m) with dry scrub or grassland vegetation; snow-covered in winter

Size: Length head/body: 47–59 in (1.2–1.5 m); tail: 35 in (90 cm). Weight: male 100–165 lb (45–75 kg); female 55–110 lb (25–50 kg)

Form: Large, long-bodied cat with thick, creamy-gray fur marked with gray rosettes; long tail and large feet also covered in fur

Diet: Wild sheep, deer, gazelles, marmots, pikas, hares, gamebirds, and livestock (sheep and goats); attacks or ambushes prey at night

Breeding: Two or 3 cubs born in spring or early summer. Lives up to 15 years in captivity

Related endangered species: Javan leopard (*Panthera pardus melas*) CR; clouded leopard (*Neofelis nebulosa*) VU; jaguar (*P. onca*) NT

Status: IUCN EN

several different individuals, both male and female, may occupy much the same home range. By leaving clear scent marks or scrapes made by scratching the ground with the hind claws, neighbors warn each other of their whereabouts and avoid meeting most of the time. Males and females will join up to mate between December and March, but go their separate ways soon afterward. The female creates a cozy den, usually a rocky shelter lined with clumps of molted fur. About three and a half months after mating, she gives birth to a litter of cubs. There may be just a single cub, or as many as five, but usually two or three.

Opportunist Predators

Hunting for its winter fur has been a major factor in the snow leopard's decline. However, the international trade in skins is now banned, and the leopard has been given legal protection by the governments of the countries in which it lives. As a predator it has also suffered from a reduction in the numbers of wild mammals (such as deer, hares, and marmots) brought about by increased farming and also an upsurge in the numbers of grazing animals such as sheep and goats. Given the opportunity, snow leopards will kill domestic animals, which leads to persecution by farmers. Nevertheless, the overall level of predation is probably not as high as local people think. A different view is taken in Tibet, where the Buddhist faith forbids the deliberate killing of any animal. Snow leopards that approach villages or farms there are usually driven away with shouts and small stones. Despite the fact that snow leopards sometimes live in close proximity to human settlements, there are no records of one ever becoming a man-eater.

Snow leopards *usually live at altitudes higher than 9,840 feet (3,000 meters). Their principal prey are the bharal (blue sheep) and the Siberian ibex.*

Great Indian Rhinoceros

Rhinoceros unicornis

Despite its armor-plated appearance, the single-horned great Indian rhinoceros is vulnerable and has suffered badly from hunting as well as from habitat loss; it is now restricted to a handful of game reserves.

The Indian rhinoceros likes wet places where it can wallow in mud during hot weather, and where sufficient food is available to support its huge bulk. It feeds and shelters in the long scrub and grass habitats found on the wide plains that fringe the rivers of northern India. However, such fertile areas also make prime farmland, and over the last 300 years the rhino's habitat has been increasingly cultivated to grow crops. The expansion of human activity quickly proved incompatible with the continued presence of the animals, which not only ate vast amounts but could also be very aggressive, especially females with young calves to protect. As a result, the rhinos were forced out of their ancestral breeding grounds. For a while, there was even a government bounty paid for each rhino killed, as a measure to reduce the damage they caused in new tea plantations.

There were other motives for killing the rhinos. In India, as elsewhere, animals were slaughtered and their horns sold to the oriental medicine trade. In addition, many were killed by both Indian and European hunters for trophies; one maharajah (Hindu prince) is said to have shot over 200 animals in 30 years.

By the beginning of the 20th century the rhinos had gone from Pakistan and northwestern India and were becoming scarce in other parts of their range. About a dozen were left in what is now the Kaziranga National Park, and a few isolated individuals survived in other parts of India. There were only about 50 left in Nepal, where the species faced imminent extinction. Since that time, however, strict protection and the careful management of sanctuaries have slowly allowed the rhinos to recover. Yet there is still too little habitat for their numbers to build

DATA PANEL

Great Indian rhinoceros

Rhinoceros unicornis

Family: Rhinocerotidae

World population: 2,575 (2007 estimate), including 2,200 in India; increasing

Distribution: Bhutan, Nepal, and parts of northern India (Assam). Now extinct in Bangladesh

Habitat: Marshy areas of long grass; various types of forest

Size: Length head/body: 12–12.5 ft (3.6–3.8 m); tail: 28–32 in (70–80 cm); height at shoulder: 5.6–6 ft (1.7–1.8 m). Weight: 3,300–4,400 lb (1,500–2,000 kg); males can weigh up to 4,840 lb (2,200 kg)

Form: A huge animal whose knobby-looking skin hangs in large, stiff sections like sheets of armor plate. There is only 1 horn, up to 20 in (52 cm) long

Diet: Grasses, leaves, and aquatic plants; sometimes raids crops

Breeding: A single calf is born after a gestation of nearly 16 months. Weaning takes more than 1 year, and young are born only once every 3 years. Females can breed at 4 years, but males take 9 years to reach maturity. Life span about 40 years

Related endangered species: Black rhinoceros (*Diceros bicornis*) CR; white rhinoceros (*Ceratotherium simum*) NT; Javan rhinoceros (*Rhinoceros sondaicus*) CR; Sumatran rhinoceros (*Dicerorhinus sumatrensis*) CR

Status: IUCN VU

up to any great extent, and illegal hunting is also difficult to stamp out. Rhino horns still fetch large sums of money, a huge temptation for poor villagers who cannot easily make a living from farming. In addition, the skin and blood of the rhinos are said to have medicinal properties, further increasing the poachers' financial rewards.

Action against Poaching

In the early 1990s large amounts of money from local sources and international conservation organizations enabled India and Nepal to implement action against poachers. Fines were introduced for traders in rhino body parts, and there were heavy jail sentences for hunters; several poachers were even shot. About 500 rhinos now live in Nepal, many of them guarded by armed soldiers in Chitwan National Park.

Great Indian rhinos *are powerful animals with massive folds of skin that hang like sheets of armor plating. Their marshy grassland habitat provides them with the food, water, and shelter they need. The fertile soil is also ideal for farming, and the rhinos are being forced out. Major floods recently drowned many rhinos in areas near big rivers.*

The Indian government protects its rhinos, too. Kaziranga National Park contains more than 1,000 animals, though it is feared that such a heavy concentration could lead to disease spreading more rapidly. To reduce the risk of an epidemic sweeping through the population, it is important that the rhinos are more widely dispersed. One aim is to reintroduce small populations to more distant areas. A pair of rhinos has been introduced to Lal Suhanra National Park in Pakistan, but the animals have not bred.

Siberian Musk Deer

Moschus moschiferus

Siberian musk deer are small, solitary, mountain-dwelling creatures that have been ruthlessly hunted for their musk—a highly valued ingredient in medicines and perfumes.

The Siberian musk deer lives alone, not in herds. It is small in stature and inhabits forests in mountain regions from Siberia to the Himalaya. The deer are mainly nocturnal, coming into the open to feed at night. In summer they may travel to higher altitudes to feed, retreating when the snows begin in the fall. However, individuals rarely travel far during their normal activities. Musk deer have a keen sense of hearing, and the males are strongly territorial.

The deer have large ears and a short tail. Neither sex has antlers, but males have sharp, downward-pointing tusks (canine teeth) that are often more than 4 inches (10 cm) long.

Like many animals that live in dense undergrowth, musk deer rely heavily on scent to leave messages for others of their species, since it is impossible to see for any distance. They smear the scent on to rocks and logs, and it is also deposited with droppings and urine. Musk—one of the scents—is produced only by the males. Sexually mature males produce the musk from a pocket on the belly, and it probably serves to attract potential mates.

Worth its Weight...

A brownish, waxy substance, musk was widely believed to have important healing properties and was used for medicinal purposes in Europe and Asia. Later it became a component of high-quality perfumes and soaps, although nowadays a synthetic substitute can be used. Up to 1 ounce (28 g) of musk could be extracted from

---

DATA PANEL

Siberian musk deer

Moschus moschiferus

Family: Moschidae

World population: More than 200,000, but spread over a huge area

Distribution: Siberia, Manchuria, Korea, China, and Sakhalin Island; some in Mongolia

Habitat: Mountain forests up to 5,000 ft (1,600 m) above sea level

Size: Length: 30–36 in (76.2–91 cm); height: 20–21 in (50–55 cm); males often smaller than

females. Weight: 24–30 lb (11–14 kg)

Form: Hind legs longer than forelegs, so the rump is higher than the shoulders, and the back appears arched. The coat is spotted when young, but adults are a dark grayish brown. They have no antlers. Males have sharp canine teeth that project downward as tusks

Diet: Mostly lichens, but also leaves, conifer needles, and tree bark. In summer a wide range of small herbaceous plants; also some grasses

Breeding: Breeding season November–December; 1 or (rarely) 2 young born in June

of the following year. Can live up to 20 years in captivity

Related endangered species: Forest musk deer (*Moschus berezovskii*) LRnt; black musk deer (*M. fuscus*) LRnt; *M. chrysogaster* (no common name) LRnt

Status: IUCN VU

Siberian musk deer *have no antlers. The male (left) has long, downward-pointing canine teeth, and the young have a spotted coat (right).*

a single animal, and although musk can be taken from a living animal, it was easier to shoot the deer than capture them alive. The extract fetched high prices, sometimes as much as its own weight in gold. The golf-ball sized pouch in which the musk is contained was also considered valuable. In one year over 100,000 glands were imported into Japan; in another more than 80,000 were exported from Russia to China. Between 1990 and 2001, 25,000 adult males were killed. Nowadays international trade is prohibited, but black market activities continue.

Although the females do not produce musk, it is hard for the hunters to avoid killing them by mistake, so populations are reduced. As a result of hunting, the species has already become extinct in some areas. The total population is thought to have halved during the 1990s; it is still in decline today. Predators, particularly lynx, take many deer, especially the young as they lie beneath the dense foliage of fir trees in early summer. Added to this, forests have been cleared for timber and fuel, and to make way for farmland, grazing animals, and roads. There is still enough of the habitat left to support several hundred thousand musk deer, but the numbers are declining.

Siberian musk deer do not breed well in captivity, so farming them cannot satisfy the demand for musk. Catching wild deer to remove the musk and then releasing them is also not very successful, and both activities encourage continued trade in musk. While this goes on, every musk deer is at risk.

Chinese Water Deer

Hydropotes inermis

Originally occupying areas of Korea and the Yangtze River Basin in China, the Chinese water deer has been introduced to England and France. The European deer populations are now more secure than their Asian relatives, which are threatened by development, shooting, and trapping.

The Chinese water deer lives in the swamps of eastern central China; a separate subspecies is found in similar habitats in Korea. Although water deer frequent reedbeds and wet places, they prefer dry land.

Unlike many deer, Chinese water deer live alone and do not form herds, although some may remain together as small family groups. Males defend their territories vigorously, especially during the winter mating season. Rival males stand side by side and try to use their tusks (they do not have antlers) to inflict serious wounds on each other.

The deer are active mainly at dusk and dawn, hiding away in dense vegetation for the rest of the day. Water deer can swim well and often do so in order to reach feeding or resting places on islands or across rivers. Their digestion is relatively inefficient, so they must select their food carefully, avoiding coarse fibrous materials. When frightened, water deer make a loud bark and leap away in high bounds.

Multiple Threats

In China the deer are frequently trapped as pests, since they raid crops. However, they are also considered valuable because the female's colostrum (a thin, milky secretion produced by the mother for the first few days after her young are born, before true lactation begins) is believed to have medicinal properties. Killing the mother to obtain the substance results in the death of offspring as well.

The deer are also threatened by development. As more and more land is taken up by farms, roads, and towns, people have squeezed out many wild animals.

DATA PANEL

Chinese water deer

Hydropotes inermis

Family: Cervidae

World population: More than 30,000

Distribution: Yangtze River Basin in China; Korea; introduced to England and France

Habitat: Reedbeds in wet places; also dry land

Size: Length head/body: 3–3.5 ft (90–95 cm); tail: 2 in (6.5 cm); height: 18–22 in (45–55 cm). Weight: 30–35 lb (14–16 kg)

Form: Small, golden-brown deer with white belly. Face short and rounded. Sleek and slender in summer, but more thickset appearance in winter, owing to long, dense coat. Fur stiff and bristly with hollow, brittle hairs that break easily. Prominent tusks in male, but no antlers. Young are dark brown with white spots and stripes

Diet: Mostly sedges (grasslike plants); also reeds, flowers, and shrubs such as brambles

Breeding: Breeds when only a few months old; usually 1 or 2 young per family, but up to 4 possible; born May–July. May live up to 12 years

Related endangered species: Bawean deer *(Axis kuhlii)* CR; Père David's deer *(Elaphurus davidianus)* EW

Status: IUCN VU

In 1990 there were estimated to be only about 10,000 water deer left in China. The status of those in Korea is unknown, but the animals are unlikely to be any more secure. The decline is partly a result of recent famines in North Korea, when many forms of wildlife were eaten by humans. However, water deer breed well in captivity; a few were released in central France in 1954 and are still present in the wild.

Escape into the Wild

There are also wild Chinese water deer in England originating from a captive herd in Woburn Park, Bedfordshire. In the 1890s animals brought from China to England by the Duke of Bedford bred successfully, and soon there were more than 100 of them. Some were transferred to the nearby Whipsnade wild animal park in 1929. They bred very successfully and many escaped into the surrounding countryside, where their numbers increased even more. In about 1950

Chinese water deer were deliberately released on the fens (lowlying flat land) of Cambridgeshire in eastern England. They bred successfully there as well and spread from this area. By 2013 the English population was 10,000 and believed to be increasing still.

Since they do little harm and have few predators, the English population seems secure and is in less danger than the original Chinese population. The species' success poses a dilemma because introduced species often become pests and, by international agreement, are supposed to be eliminated in their nonnative countries. However, perhaps the Chinese water deer living in England should be left alone in case the native Asian populations become even more seriously endangered in the future.

The Chinese water deer *has coarse, brittle hair that breaks easily. Males have tusks but no antlers, and females (below) have neither antlers nor tusks.*

Blackbuck

Antilope cervicapra

Once widespread and abundant on the plains of India, the blackbuck has gradually been squeezed out by a rapidly expanding human population.

Blackbuck are herd animals that live in groups of up to 50 individuals. Each herd consists of a single male accompanied by a "harem" of females. Blackbuck are mainly active during the day. In the dry season, however—when it is very hot—they seek shade and are most active around dawn and dusk. Like other herd animals that live out on open grasslands, blackbuck are very alert to danger and have extremely keen eyesight. If alarmed, one individual may leap into the air, startling the rest of the herd, which then gallop away.

Quick Escapes

Blackbuck can actually run quite fast, up to 40 mph (65 km/h), and can keep going for many miles. This outpaces most predators, so they are only likely to be killed by ambush or a very persistent hunter on horseback. For years muskets, and later rifles, posed a lethal threat to the blackbuck, which were heavily hunted for sport and for their meat and skins. Farmers also kill the animals because they raid crops. Blackbuck are especially fond of sorghum and millet, and a small herd can eat a significant amount, depriving peasant farmers of food and income. Farmers often employ children to scare the blackbuck away, but they also set traps to kill the animals.

Blackbuck prefer flat land away from trees and were once the prevalent large mammal in this type of habitat. But people, too, realized the potential of the plains and expanded into them,

DATA PANEL

Blackbuck

Antilope cervicapra

Family: Bovidae

World population: About 50,000 in India, and increasing; introduced populations of 8,600 in Argentina and 35,000 in the United States

Distribution: India, Nepal, Pakistan; already extinct in Bangladesh

Habitat: Open grasslands

Size: Length: about 42 in (1.2 m); height at shoulder: 30–34 in (75–85 cm). Weight: 70–92 lb (32–42 kg)

Form: Graceful, medium-sized

antelope with brownish back; coat color varies regionally and is generally paler later in the season. Both sexes have a contrasting white belly and white inside legs; both also have white ring around eye. The male (only) has horns that are about 2 ft long (60 cm) and twisted through approximately 4 turns

Diet: Blackbuck feed on grasses and crops, nibbled delicately with their narrow, sheeplike muzzle

Breeding: The males become very aggressive and territorial in the breeding season, which usually occurs March–April. However, breeding can occur

at any time. A single calf is born each year and weaned at 6 months. Adults are mature at 2 years. Life span 10–12 years, occasionally up to 18

Related endangered species: No close relatives, but some other species of gazelles and antelope are threatened

Status: IUCN NT

transforming large areas into farmland. One naturalist estimated that there were perhaps 80,000 blackbuck living in India only 50 years ago. By the mid-1970s only 22,000–24,000 remained, mostly in protected areas. However, conservation measures enabled the population to rise to 50,000 by 2001 and the species' numbers are now stable.

Blackbuck breed quite well in captivity, and they are kept in many zoos and wildlife parks. They have also been introduced to the United States and to Argentina, where they do well on game ranches. Sometimes they are kept just because they are attractive animals. Elsewhere they are hunted for

trophies and meat. Since they are not native American mammals, they are not protected by normal game laws and can be shot at any time. While some people are unhappy about this, hunting does provide an incentive to keep and breed the blackbuck, making it less likely that they will become extinct. This is a valuable conservation safety net, bearing in mind the increasing human population in India and the need for more land to farm there.

Blackbuck males *have distinctive twisted horns that are about 2 feet (60 cm) long. In parts of their range they are pursued by trophy hunters and killed for meat.*

Gaur

Bos gaurus

Pressures of habitat loss and hunting have brought the gaur to crisis point. Scientists have succeeded in producing a baby gaur—the first endangered animal ever to have been cloned.

The enormous gaur is a tropical equivalent of the yak or bison. Its massive, muscular body is accentuated in males by a large shoulder hump. The thickness of the bull gaur's neck is enhanced by a large flap of skin, called a dewlap, dangling from the throat between the chin and the chest. A shaggy mane like that of a bull yak would be impractical for a gaur, since it needs to keep cool in the tropical heat and spends much of its time pushing through dense vegetation that would snag long hair.

Both male and female gaurs are armed with large, upcurved horns, joined across the top of the head by a prominent brow ridge. The horns look fearsome, but gaurs rarely use them for fighting. Disputes over females occur between rival males, but most of the time they are settled by displays. They give the rivals a chance to size each other up, and the inferior male usually backs off. Females are even less aggressive, and the average gaur mother loses at least half her offspring to the species' main predator, the tiger.

Gaurs sometimes live in herds of up to 40 animals, though groups of 10 to15 are more usual. Most herds consist of females and young with one mature male. Immature males roam in bachelor groups, awaiting the opportunity to take over a herd of their own. Most births occur between December and June, and young gaurs are integrated into the herd soon afterward. Being part of a herd is a gaur's best defense against predators—there is safety in numbers. At the first sign of danger a gaur will alert the herd by giving a snorting alarm, while standing still and facing the direction of the threat. If the attack continues, the gaur begins to run, sending out further warnings in the form of vibrations as it pounds the ground.

Competition

Predation by tigers is a significant factor in the gaur's decline, but it is difficult to know

DATA PANEL

Gaur

Bos gaurus

Family: Bovidae

World population: 13,000–30,000

Distribution: India, Bhutan, China, Indochina, and Malay Peninsula

Habitat: Tropical thickets and forests

Size: Length: 8.2–11 ft (2.5–3.3 m); height at shoulder: 5.5–7.2 ft (1.7–2.2 m). Weight: 1,540–2,200 lb (700–1,000 kg)

Form: Massive, powerfully built ox with short, dark brown hair and curved horns linked by prominent brow ridge

Diet: Grasses, bamboo, other shoots, and fruit

Breeding: One, occasionally 2 calves born between June and December. Life span up to 30 years

Related endangered species: Wild yak (*Bos mutus*) VU; banteng (*B. javanicus*) EN; kouprey (*B. sauveli*) CR; mountain anoa (*Bubalus quarlesi*) EN

Status: IUCN VU

how to tackle the problem without harming the tigers, which are also endangered. It makes better sense to address the other main problem facing the gaur: the expansion of human settlement and livestock farming. Gaurs and domestic cattle compete for the same food; and when domestic herds move in, the gaurs retreat. Where their daily routine is disturbed by people, gaurs become virtually nocturnal.

First Clone

There is no doubt that the gaur is facing a crisis. Several zoos are participating in a species-recovery program, but at the start of the 21st century captive stocks were so low that scientists in Iowa took the drastic step of cloning a gaur. Genetic material—DNA—taken from the skin of a dead gaur was inserted into a cow's egg from which the cow DNA had been removed. The egg was then implanted into the womb of an ordinary cow, where it developed into a normal gaur calf. The calf, named Noah, is the first endangered animal ever to have been cloned. Sadly, Noah died within two days.

The arrival of Noah has stirred up a lot of debate. Because clones can be made from dead animals, some people believe that the same techniques could be used to resurrect extinct species. Others say that cloning is unethical and that populations of clones lack the genetic diversity needed to make them stable; the genetic diversity of captive gaur herds already has to be closely monitored to prevent inbreeding.

The gaur has never been particularly common largely due to the patchy nature of its habitat and its apparent vulnerability to predation.

Takin

Budorcas taxicolor

The takin is struggling to survive in the wild areas around the foothills of the Himalaya. It is preyed on not only by wolves and bears, but also by humans for its meat. The combined pressures of predation and habitat destruction have taken a severe toll on numbers.

The takin is also known as the golden-fleeced cow, the gnu-goat, and the chamois cattle, an indication that it is a difficult animal to classify. It shares many physical characteristics with other members of the Bovidae family, which include sheep, goats, cattle, and antelopes.

The takin's shaggy coat and short, powerful legs are adaptations to the harsh mountainous landscapes of southwestern China, Tibet, Myanmar (Burma), and northern India where it is still found. There are four subspecies of takin found in different parts of the range, but all are under pressure from the loss of habitat and from competition for food with domestic livestock that eat huge amounts of vegetation.

Hunting for meat is still a major threat to the takin. The animal has a stocky body, which makes it attractive quarry for any hunter. It has been hunted for centuries by humans; the animals are caught in snares and pitfall traps or are killed with spears and guns. The takin's natural predators are wolves and bears.

Balancing Act

The takin has remarkable feet, similar to those of a yak, with broad cloven hooves that splay to give grip on rocky ground. In addition, there is a kind of spur, or highly developed dewclaw. The dewclaw in most bovids is small and insignificant, having been reduced from the ancestral thumb. In the takin, however, this otherwise redundant digit has been reinstated and now serves as a useful third toe, helping the animal maintain its balance in the rocky landscapes.

Takin live in small herds and appear to be wilier than many of their close relatives; they are certainly more cunning than their domestic equivalents, goats, for example. At the first sign of danger takin raise the alarm with a loud, coughing snort, at which the entire herd will head for cover. They cannot

DATA PANEL

Takin

Budorcas taxicolor

Family: Bovidae

World population: Unknown, but more than 5,000 in China; decreasing

Distribution: Tibet, Myanmar (Burma), parts of central and southern China, Bhutan, and the Assam and Sikkim regions of India

Habitat: Mountain slopes between 3,300 and 15,000 ft (1,000–4,500 m) at upper limit of trees

Size: Length: 5.5–7.2 ft (1.7–2.3 m); height at shoulder: up to 3.3–4.3 ft (1–1.3 m); females about 20% smaller than males. Weight: up to 790 lb (350 kg)

Form: A dumpy, cowlike animal with a dense shaggy coat, stumpy legs, and broad feet. Both sexes bear sturdy, backward-pointing horns

Diet: Browses leaves from deciduous trees and shrubs; also grazes grasses and herbs

Breeding: Calves born singly (twins rare) in March after gestation of 7–8 months. Life span up to 15 years

Related endangered species: Mountain anoa (*Bubalus quarlesi*) EN; wild yak (*Bos mutus*) VU; kouprey (*B. sauveli*) CR; gaur (*B. gaurus*) VU; other wild cattle

Status: IUCN VU

run particularly fast, but their yellowish-brown coat offers effective camouflage, especially when the animals lie down among dense grasses.

Scent and Taste

Takin do not have specialized scent glands, yet scent is an important part of their lives, a trait that makes them more similar to goats than to other wild cattle. The animals secrete a smelly, oily substance from their skin and spray urine all over the underside of their body, which enhances their personal scent for others to interpret. Hormones in the urine may help advertise the breeding condition of an individual.

The takin *is found around the tree line in the Himalayan foothills. It lives in small herds of between 10 and 15 animals.*

Another goatlike characteristic of the takin is its very broad diet. The animals will eat just about any plant material, favoring leaves and tender shoots, but they will also eat tough and even woody material if no alternative is available. If food is above head height, takin rear on their hind legs to reach it, something cattle do not do. Salt is also important in the takin's diet, and the animals travel long distances to find places where they can lick naturally occurring salt deposits.

Nilgiri Tahr

Nilgiritragus hylocrius

A close relative of the Himalayan tahr, the fairly large Nilgiri tahr is found only on a very few hilltops of the Western Ghats mountains in southern India.

The Nilgiri tahr lives high up in the Western Ghats mountains of southern India, in a landscape of rolling hills and dramatic cliffs. The animals are more or less confined to altitudes of 4,000–8,500 feet (1,220–2,590 m). The barely accessible ledges where the tahr spends much of its time have the significant advantage of being relatively safe from predators. Killing by other animals does not seem to have been a major factor in the tahr's decline. There are hardly any tigers or leopards left in its range, and even the adaptable Asian wild dog, the dhole, does not appear to favor tahr as prey.

Apparently, young tahr make very good eating, but the meat of old males is barely edible. If they were not so rare, Nilgiri tahrs could be an important source of meat protein for undernourished local people.

Population Management

Hunting may seem like the last thing such an endangered animal would need, but there is some evidence to suggest that the tahr were better off when their habitat was managed by local hunting associations. In the days of the hunt access was strictly restricted so that numbers of game animals were allowed to build up for the sport of a few privileged members. Later, when the management passed from the hunting clubs to the overstretched government forest department, things deteriorated fast. Even though the tahr was officially protected, access to its habitat was easy and largely unrestricted, so many animals were poached for meat. This sort of unmanaged exploitation caused a rapid population decline, whereas carefully managed harvesting could have maintained secure and healthy populations.

Wild tahr do not like disturbance; and although few people or livestock venture on to the precipitous cliffs where they live, crops such as tea, cardamom, plantain, and wattle are planted right up to the cliff edges,

DATA PANEL

Nilgiri tahr (Nilgiri ibex)

Nilgiritragus hylocrius

Family: Bovidae

World population: 1,800–2,000 (2008 estimate)

Distribution: Scattered populations in highlands of southern India

Habitat: Steep, grassy and tree-covered slopes and cliffs at altitudes of 4,000–8,500 ft (1,220–2,590 m)

Size: Length head/body: 36–54 in (90–140 cm); tail: 3.5–4.5 in (9–12 cm); height at shoulder: 24–40 in (60–106 cm). Weight: 110–220 lb (50–100 kg); bucks heavier than does

Form: Brownish goat; males are darker than females and have a pale saddle patch

Diet: Mostly grasses and leaves

Breeding: One (occasionally 2) kids born at any time of year

Related endangered species:
Arabian tahr (*Arabitragus jayakari*) EN; Himalayan tahr (*Hemitragus jemlahicus*) NT

Status: IUCN EN

INDIA

SRI LANKA

and cattle are grazed on almost every other available patch of land. The comings and goings of plantation workers and livestock disturb the tahr, and restrict their activities to small patches of inaccessible habitat surrounded by areas of farmland.

It became clear that the tahr was in need of help in the mid-1970s, when surveys indicated that the total wild population had dropped to about 1,000 animals. In some areas this represented a 97 percent decline in only 30 years. Conservationists were appalled, and just in time several areas were declared sanctuaries for the tahr. Fortunately, even though tahr populations are still extremely small, they seem to have a good mixture of ages and sexes, and the birth rate is relatively high.

The dramatic scenery in which the Nilgiri tahr lives has always made the area a popular retreat from the hot lowlands, and the growing tourist industry is showing signs of becoming a major positive factor in the tahr's survival. If tourists can be drawn to an area for its scenery and wildlife, the benefits of conserving rare species will begin to outweigh those of farming, or even poaching, and the tahr may stand a reasonable chance of recovery.

Plantations are now managed with the tahr's welfare in mind, and in some places the animals have overcome their fear of people. Semitame herds are becoming an important tourist attraction. With careful management there is no reason why the Nilgiri tahr should not once again roam the hills and cliffs of the Western Ghats range in substantial numbers.

This Nilgiri tahr *can be recognized as a male by its pale saddle patch.*

Nubian Ibex

Capra nubiana

Life is a struggle at the best of times for all desert mammals. The plight of the Nubian ibex has been made worse by trophy hunting.

Nubian ibex are skilled *at climbing the rocky slopes of desert mountains.*

Nubian ibex inhabit the rocky slopes of desert mountains in the Middle East, the Arabian Peninsula, and northeastern Africa. The adults are often found living alone (especially males). Females, with their young, including immature males (less than three years old), may form small groups. The ibex walks slowly among the rocks and across open slopes, searching for grasses, shoots, and leaves to eat. Like other ruminants, they will rest periodically to chew their cud before moving on in search of more food.

The Nubian is smaller than most other ibex, and the only one that is mainly adapted to life in desert conditions. Its pale, shiny coat reflects the sun's rays, helping keep the animal cool. This means that ibex can remain active even during the hottest parts of the day and wander widely in search of food.

Although there are no mammalian predators to fear in the desert, eagles and other birds of prey present a danger. Normally the ibex stay out in the open where there are plenty of escape routes and are ready to use their speed to escape attack should the need arise.

DATA PANEL

Nubian ibex

Capra nubiana

Family: Bovidae

World population: Fewer than 2,500

Distribution: Israel, Jordan, Oman, Saudi Arabia, Yemen, Egypt, northeastern Sudan

Habitat: Slopes of desert mountains

Size: Length: 42–48 in (107–122 cm); height at shoulder: 24–30 in (60–75 cm). Weight: 55–150 lb (25–70 kg)

Form: A goatlike animal, sandy brown with paler hindquarters. Mature males have a dark beard and a black stripe down the back and also up the front of each foreleg. The horns sweep upward and backward in a semicircular direction, each with up to 36 prominent knobbly ridges across the outer surface of the curve. Male horns may grow to 4 ft (1.2 m); in females they are thinner and less than 14 in (35 cm) long. The young have white underparts.

Diet: Almost any type of vegetation

Breeding: Mates in late summer (or October), producing a single kid after 5-month gestation. Twins are rare. Breeds only once a year, from the age of 2–3 years onward. Life span at least 17 years

Related endangered species: Walia ibex (*Capra walie*) EN; markhor (*Capra falconeri*) EN

Status: IUCN VU

However, in winter it can become quite cold, especially at night, when the clear skies rapidly absorb heat from the ground, and the temperature drops. At these times the ibex may seek shelter in ravines and caves. Similarly, when it rains, the animals will try to avoid getting wet.

Threats from Hunters

The ibex is prized for its meat by local people in the countries where it is found, especially since few other animals in the desert are big enough for humans to eat. In contrast to most desert animals, the Nubian ibex likes to drink daily, so it rarely lives far from water. It can be relatively easily shot or snared as it approaches water holes, especially since these are often in clefts between rock faces and only accessible via narrow tracks. In addition, wars have frequently been fought in regions where the ibex live, and the animals would have been a welcome source of food to soldiers, who were able to kill them with their powerful rifles. Moreover, the prominent curved horns of the ibex have attracted attention from trophy hunters, who seek out big males to shoot.

Like other large desert mammals, the Nubian ibex was probably always scarce, but hunting has made it even more so. There are none left in Syria, Lebanon, or (probably) Egypt, and the few animals that remain elsewhere are scattered over a very large area and live in widely separated small groups.

Between 1998 and 2006, captive-bred animals were released into the Wadi Mujib Nature Reserve in Jordan to bolster a small and declining population. By 2006, the population there was estimated to be 200. Numbers are stable in Israel and Egypt, but may be declining in Saudi Arabia.

Markhor

Capra falconeri

The impressive markhor, once common in the southern foothills of the Himalaya, has become rare in the wild as a direct result of centuries of hunting for its meat and its magnificent horns.

The markhor is the world's largest goat and one of the most unusual-looking. Sadly, it is also one of the rarest. In the mid-20th century, herds numbering well over 100 individuals were relatively common in the scrubby woodlands on the lower slopes of the western Himalaya. Today, however, the largest herds rarely exceed 30 markhors, with an average herd made up of just nine animals.

The herds move up and down the mountains with the seasons, reaching up to 13,000 feet (3,940 m) in midsummer but returning to 2,000 to 3,000 feet (610 to 910 m) to escape the worst of the winter weather. The largest herds consist of females and their offspring. Young markhors may stay with their mothers for up to two and a half years; their early lives are fraught with danger, with over 50 percent disappearing, presumed dead, in their first 18 months.

An adult male markhor in its winter breeding coat is a magnificent animal, with a shaggy mane around the neck and chest, and flowing "trousers" of long hair growing on the legs. The female has rather less flamboyant fringes of hair, but both sexes go back to a shorter, sleeker coat in summer.

A Horny Problem

Undoubtedly the most remarkable features of the markhor are their splendid horns, which are present in both sexes. Unlike the antlers grown by male deer, the horns of goats and cattle are not cast off after the breeding season, but continue to grow throughout the animal's life. A huge pair of horns is therefore an unmistakable sign of a healthy and long-lived individual. The largest horns ever recorded were 5.3 feet (1.6 m) long, almost as long as the body of the

goat that grew them. The horns of the female markhor rarely exceed 10 inches (25 cm) in length.

Despite being an obvious symbol of longevity and vigor, the male's horns are not just for show. They also make very effective weapons. Rival males lock horns and try to unbalance their opponent by shoving and twisting. Deadly earnest though the battles appear, such bouts tend to be tests of brute strength rather than genuine fights to the death, and a vanquished male will usually live to fight another day.

Sadly, however, the very horns that might make a particular male successful at winning mates may well be his undoing. Although strictly illegal, the trade in markhor horns is highly lucrative. Powdered horn is used in many traditional medicines, and a set of mounted horns makes a valuable hunting trophy. In China markhor horn changes hands for large sums of money. It is not surprising that some impoverished local people view the markhor as simply a larger and potentially more valuable version of their own domestic goats and are willing to supply the black market.

Habitat Competition

Markhors also have their fair share of nonhuman predators, including wolves, snow leopards, and lynxes. In addition, steady encroachment of human settlement within the markhor's range and competition from domestic livestock for the limited grazing available make life difficult.

Of the three distinct subspecies of markhor, all are Endangered, and one, the Turkmenian markhor, is Critically Endangered. Even without the threat of habitat loss and illegal hunting, life is tough for the markhors. The animal's diet is relatively poor in

DATA PANEL

Markhor

Capra falconeri

Family: Bovidae

World population: Fewer than 2,500

Distribution: Himalayan regions of Afghanistan, Pakistan, India, Tajikistan, Uzbekistan, and Turkmenistan

Habitat: Scrubby woodland on mountain slopes

Size: Length: up to 6.2 ft (1.9 m); height to shoulder: up to 3.7 ft (1.2 m); females smaller than males. Weight: up to 242 lb (110 kg)

Form: Large shaggy-coated, pale brown goat with distinctive corkscrewlike horns

Diet: Grass, leaves, twigs, and mast (nuts, including acorns)

Breeding: Between 1 and 3 kids born April–June. Life span at least 15 years

Related endangered species: Nubian ibex *(Capra nubiana)* EN; walia ibex *(C. walia)* CR; various other wild goats

Status: IUCN EN

nutrients, especially in winter, when they switch from grazing tussocky grasses to browsing twigs and leaves. In order to eat enough to survive, a typical markhor will spend between eight and 12 hours a day feeding, pausing briefly at midday to rest and chew cud. Such a regime ensures the most effective possible digestion of its tough food.

The name "markhor," *translated literally from the Persian, means "snake-eater." The goats are vegetarian, but they will kill snakes in self-defense, and it is presumably from this that the name comes.*

Temminck's Tragopan

Tragopan temminckii

The fantastic adornments and bizarre courtship dance of the male Temminck's tragopan make it one of the most astonishing of all the pheasants. It is one of the few that seems to be in no immediate danger, although it suffers the effects of hunting, habitat destruction, and sheer ignorance.

It is a paradox that some of the most glamorous, extravagantly plumed, and ornamented of all birds—the pheasants—should also be among the most mysterious and elusive. A few species, such as the blue peacock, the ring-necked pheasant, and the red jungle fowl, have been domesticated and carried all over the world, but most of their wild relatives are so rarely seen and little studied that until quite recently some of the more exotic Chinese species were dismissed as figments of the imagination.

Of the 48 pheasant species all but one are confined to Asia. There they live mainly in the dense rain forests of the tropics or in the mountain forests of the Himalaya and southern China. They are furtive birds; the females are cryptically colored, and the males usually keep their most spectacular features for their courtship displays. Most males are still intensely colorful, however, which may explain why they keep to shadowy undergrowth where they are well hidden.

Feathered Glory

Most pheasants feed on the ground, but the five species of tragopan are unusual in being just as at home in the trees. This allows them to enjoy a wider variety of food, from mosses and bamboo shoots to the flowers and fruit of trees. In the fall Temminck's tragopan, the most widely distributed of the family, spends time eating the berries of trees such as rowan and viburnum found on the mountain slopes. In winter it moves downhill and switches to grasses and ferns, often digging them out from beneath the snow.

Uniquely for pheasants, tragopans also nest in the trees. Mated females make nests (from twigs, leaves, and feathers) up to 26 feet (8 m) from the forest floor. Newly hatched chicks must jump or clamber to the ground to find food. Within two or three days they are able to fly back up to perches where they roost nightly beneath their mother's wings.

The male takes no part in these domestic arrangements. He is, in any case, too conspicuous to be welcome. A mature male Temminck's tragopan is a magnificent sight, with silver-spotted crimson plumage and

---

DATA PANEL

Temminck's tragopan

Tragopan temminckii

Family: Phasianidae

World population: About 100,000 birds, but declining

Distribution: Eastern Himalaya, from India, northeastern Myanmar (Burma), and northern Vietnam to central China

Habitat: Dense evergreen or mixed forest with rhododendron or bamboo thickets

Size: Length: male 25 in (64 cm); female 23 in (58 cm). Weight: male 3 lb (1.4 kg); female 2.2 lb (1 kg)

Form: Plump gamebird with short, rounded wings, strong legs, and a moderate-length, rounded tail. Male deep red with pearly gray spots below; has inflatable blue-and-red lappet (flap) and erectile horns. Female gray-brown above, mottled black; pale brown with black patches and pale spots below

Diet: Mainly leaves, grasses, ferns, bamboo shoots, flowers, berries, and seeds; occasionally insects

Breeding: Male often polygamous (has many sexual partners); female nests alone in trees in May–June, incubating 3–5 eggs for 3.5–4 weeks. Chicks fledge within about 14 days

Related endangered species: Blyth's tragopan (*Tragopan blythii*) VU; Cabot's tragopan (*T. caboti*) VU; western tragopan (*T. melanocephalus*) VU

Status: IUCN LC

CHINA

INDIA
MYANMAR
LAOS
THAILAND
CAMBODIA
VIETNAM
PHILIPPINES
TAIWAN

overlapping silver disks on his breast that gleam in the forest gloom like newly minted coins. Yet even this is inadequate to win the favors of a female tragopan.

On seeing an eligible female, he slips behind a rock and then rises to peer over the top. As he does so, a lappet on his neck expands and unfurls into a flap of scarlet-patterned, electric-blue skin, while a pair of blue "horns" rise on his head. After few seconds he fans his tail and beats his wings, then starts making weird clicking and gasping sounds as he crouches behind his rock again. Then comes the climax, as he suddenly rears up on tiptoe with his wings outspread downward, hissing and inflating his lappet to its fullest extent. Stunned by this vision, the female may then allow him to mate.

Losing Ground

Few people have seen this astonishing display because the tragopan is so secretive. It is becoming a rarer sight as the bird's habitat is steadily eroded by logging and the removal of the forest understory. Small timber is cut for firewood or to provide fodder for livestock; it is denuded by browsing goats or cleared altogether for farmland. The tragopans themselves are also hunted for food—not surprising given that this large, plump pheasant has plenty of meat.

Temminck's tragopan may survive all this, for although its numbers are dwindling, it has a wide range. Other species of tragopan are more vulnerable because they are far more restricted. For example, Cabot's tragopan lives only in scattered patches of forest in southeast China. It has a population of probably fewer than 5,000 mature birds. Although classified as Vulnerable, this status may need to be upgraded to Endangered. Many other pheasants— over two-thirds of all species—are considered at risk.

Effective conservation is vital for the survival of these glorious birds, but it is hampered by a lack of data. The birds live in some of the least-known regions in the world, and in many cases their populations and even details of their lives are virtually unknown.

A male Temminck's tragopan *shows its spectacular plumage. These birds remain hidden in thick cover for most of the time.*

Baikal Teal

Anas formosa

The world population of this beautiful duck was in rapid retreat—a decline caused chiefly by hunting and the destruction of major wetland sites in its wintering range—but, especially since the year 2000, there has been a dramatic upturn in its fortunes.

The exquisite-looking Baikal teal has a very apt species name: *formosa* means "beautiful." The males are particularly handsome in their breeding plumage, while the females have a more sober charm (as with other ducks, their more muted colors provide camouflage and protection from predators while sitting on the nest). Baikal teal's common name refers to Lake Baikal in Siberia, the largest freshwater lake in the world (by volume). On the western fringes of the species' breeding range, the lake was where the first individuals were found by explorers in 1775.

Until the early 1900s it was one of the most numerous ducks in eastern Asia, common across much of the tundra and the boggy taiga regions of Siberia. Flocks thousands strong were regularly seen when the birds migrated to their winter quarters farther south, with particularly impressive concentrations being reported from Japan, a major wintering site for the species. In the 1960s one flock of 100,000 birds was reported there; another was estimated to be about 2 miles (3 km) long.

Rapid Decline

In the 1960s and 1970s, however, ornithologists detected a major decline in numbers of Baikal teal. Decades of shooting and trapping were probably the main factors that brought about this situation. Early in the winter of 1947, for example, just three hunters in southwestern Japan took a reported 50,000 Baikal teal, including some 10,000 birds in a single day. By the 1980s it was thought that the Korean population had fallen to around 20,000. Hunting still poses a serious threat, but it has declined greatly.

In addition to shooting, poisoned grain is used to kill the ducks in China and mortality can be high, since the species gathers in large flocks on arable land

DATA PANEL

Baikal teal

Anas formosa

Family: Anatidae

World population: More than 1 million, increasing

Distribution: Breeds in eastern Siberia; migrates through Mongolia and North Korea; winters mainly in Japan, South Korea, China, Taiwan

Habitat: Breeds in open meadows with grass tussocks near water and in bogs with mosses and clumps of willow and larch; winters on lakes and reservoirs and on farmland

Size: Length: 15–17 in (39–43 cm). Weight: 13–18 oz (360–520 g)

Form: Small, compact dabbling duck; male in breeding plumage (most of year) has striking head pattern. Female resembles females of other dabbling ducks, but more strongly spotted, especially on flanks

Diet: Grasses, sedges, water plants, algae, and crops, including grain and acorns; also snails, insects, and other aquatic invertebrates

Breeding: Begins in May; nests in single pairs or loose groups; female makes hollow concealed in vegetation; lays 6–9 pale-green eggs, which she incubates on her own for 3–3.5 weeks; ducklings fledge in 3.5–4 weeks

Related endangered species: 22 species of duck are threatened, including marbled teal (*Marmaronetta angustirostris*) VU; Eaton's pintail (*Anas eatoni*) VU; Campbell Islands teal (*A. nesiotis*) EN; brown teal (*A. chlorotis*) EN; and Madagascar teal (*A. bernieri*) EN

Status: IUCN LC

so large numbers can be killed at a time. Such direct persecution is not the whole story, however. Habitat loss is also a threat. At China's largest freshwater lake, Poyang Hu, and on the adjacent Sanjiang plain major declines have occurred not just because of hunting but also as a result of drainage and alteration of habitat for agriculture. Wintering sites in South Korea, too, are threatened by the drainage and development of wetlands. Offsetting this, newly reclaimed land in South Korea has given Baikal teal more suitable habitat in which to spend the winter.

Although the Baikal teal is legally protected in Hong Kong, Japan, Mongolia, Russia, South Korea, and some provinces of China, it is still sometimes hunted in its wintering areas. Although some major sites—such as Lakes Bolob and Khanka in Siberia and Katano in Japan—lie within protected areas, others continue to be threatened by habitat alteration or degradation.

To ensure the teal's future, conservationists need to learn more about its decline and the threats it faces. Other targets are to put in place a management plan

The male Baikal teal's *beautiful plumage has not saved it from hunters, who once threatened its survival, though numbers have recovered dramatically in recent years.*

for the largest wintering population, in South Korea; to research the bird's status as a winter visitor in China; to control hunting of all ducks in China (even where birds are protected, they can be shot in error for more common species); and to ensure the teal is legally protected by all nations within its large range.

Encouragingly, reports of huge concentrations of Baikal teals have recently come from birders in China and especially South Korea, where coordinated counts in 2004 produced 658,000 birds, many times more than the numbers seen in the previous decade. Then, in January 2009 the winter concentration in South Korea peaked at more than 1 million. A flock of 50,000 at Yancheng Nature Reserve in the winter of 2005–06 was the biggest seen in China for many years. The future for this beautiful duck now looks much more secure.

Black-faced Spoonbill

Platalea minor

Facing an array of threats ranging from human impact on its environment to direct persecution, the black-faced spoonbill—an already rare bird—will suffer further declines unless urgent action is taken.

The black-faced spoonbill is the least known and rarest of the world's six species of spoonbill. It was once apparently common over much of its range along the coasts of eastern Asia. Today it is reduced to a small breeding population in the Far East.

Until recently its only known breeding grounds were on four small, rocky islets off the west coast of the Korean Peninsula. In June 1999 a Chinese professor visited the Changshan Islands in Korea Bay, northeastern China. There he saw three pairs of black-faced spoonbills. On a return visit he found a nest containing three chicks. Eggs from two other nests had been taken by fishers, but the birds were incubating second broods.

Although the other spoonbills are well researched, ornithologists know very little about the black-faced spoonbill's precise ecology. It is known to roost communally and, if prey is abundant enough, to feed in small flocks—up to 25 birds have been recorded feeding together during winter in Hong Kong.

The spoonbill's feeding behavior is distinctive. Wading into the shallows with the long spatulate bill partly open, the bird holds it almost vertically in the water or fine silt and sweeps it from side to side. It locates prey with the help of touch receptors in the tip of the bill; it snaps up small fish, aquatic insects and their larvae, crustaceans, and other small animals.

Breeding Sites

Black-faced spoonbills are migratory. In the fall, after rearing their young, the birds leave the breeding grounds (in temperate regions) to fly to subtropical parts of Asia for winter. Satellite tracking has shown that birds wintering in Hong Kong and Taiwan migrate along China's east coast, then cross the Yellow Sea to the Korean Peninsula. Tracking has also identified several important stopover sites in China.

In 1999 seven of 12 birds fitted with transmitters at two different wintering sites (one in Hong Kong, one in Taiwan) returned to islets off the Korean coast. This demonstrated the importance of the main breeding sites for the survival of the

DATA PANEL

Black-faced spoonbill

Platalea minor

Family: Threskiornithidae

World population: 2,693 (2012 survey)

Distribution: Breeds on islets off west coasts of North and South Korea and on one of the Changshan Islands off the coast of southeastern Liaoning Province, China. Winters as far away as Japan and the Philippines, but mainly on Tsengwen estuary, Taiwan; Inner Deep Bay, Hong Kong; and the Red River delta, Vietnam

Habitat: Breeds on offshore islets; migrates south to winter on marshes, mangroves, flooded rice fields, fish ponds, tidal mudflats, and estuaries

Size: Length: 23.5–31 in (60–78.5 cm)

Form: Medium-sized waterbird with spatula-shaped, black-tipped gray bill; long black legs. Plumage white with area of bare black skin on face and throat; yellowish band from base of neck and longer crest on nape in breeding adults; immatures similar to nonbreeding adults but with pinkish-gray bill and darker wingtip feathers

Diet: Mainly fish and aquatic mollusks; also insects and crustaceans, including shrimps and crabs

Breeding: Breeds in small colonies of 2–3 pairs; both sexes build nest of twigs on cliff ledge; 4–6 eggs laid

Related endangered species: Nine species of ibis in the family Threskiornithidae, including the northern bald ibis (*Geronticus eremita*) CR and Asian crested ibis (*Nipponia nippon*) EN

Status: IUCN EN

species. Birds have been seen at the Tumen estuary, which separates Russia and North Korea, and they bred for the first time in the neighboring Russian province of Primorye in 2006.

Four of the breeding islets in North Korea are protected as seabird sanctuaries, as are a number of wintering sites in Hong Kong, Vietnam, and Japan. The species is legally protected in China (including Hong Kong), North Korea, South Korea, and Japan.

Threatened by Industry

Despite such protection, the black-faced spoonbill faces a variety of threats, the most important being habitat destruction. The chief wintering grounds face the threat of land reclamation, particularly in China—where the booming economy has resulted in many coastal wetlands being converted to industrial sites and fish-farming ponds—and also in South Korea and Japan. Other key sites could soon be lost to industrial developments in China. In southern Taiwan developers wanted to build a huge industrial project next to the spoonbill's main wintering site at Chiku Lagoons. If the

The black-faced spoonbill, *in common with all species of spoonbill, has a remarkable bill. It is long and flattened, expanding to a spatula-shaped tip.*

scheme had gone ahead, it would have encroached onto the lagoons, and pollution from the complex could have wiped out the fish stocks that the birds depend upon. After a long campaign, the proposals were scrapped and the area is now a nature reserve.

Increasing levels of disturbance by fishers and tourists, and also hunting, are threats in China and Vietnam. Fishers in China sometimes collect waterbird eggs at nest sites. Pollution is a problem for spoonbills wintering in Hong Kong.

Conservationists have surveyed coastal wetlands in China for previously unknown wintering sites. They have also campaigned for the protection of known wintering sites (especially on Taiwan) and the new Chinese breeding sites. Assessing the spoonbill's population is difficult. Although there have been apparent increases, they may be due to increased coverage by birdwatchers rather than real growth.

Jerdon's Courser

Rhinoptilus bitorquatus

The enigmatic Jerdon's courser made ornithological history when it was rediscovered in eastern India in 1986 after being thought extinct since the early 20th century. However, it may yet be lost as a result of habitat destruction and disturbance.

The rediscovery of the rare Jerdon's courser was one of the most exciting ornithological events of recent years. The delicately built wader, with its distinctive double breast-band, was first discovered for science in about 1848 by Thomas Jerdon, a Scottish army surgeon who was one of the major pioneers of Indian ornithology.

In the 50 years following his discovery Jerdon's courser was seen and collected intermittently within a restricted area to the north of Madras in the states of Andhra Pradesh and Maharashtra, mainly between the Godavari and Penner River systems in the low mountain system of the Eastern Ghats mountains. A bird observed in the Penner River Valley in 1900 by an English ornithologist, Howard Campbell, represented the last known record of the species, and from then on Jerdon's courser was assumed to be extinct.

Inspired by the renowned Indian ornithologist Dr. Salim Ali, the Bombay Natural History Society decided to carry out investigations to discover more about the status of Jerdon's courser. Searches took place during the 1980s in the areas where the courser had previously been recorded. Although preliminary surveys could find no trace of the species, when illustrated posters were distributed to local people, a number of them claimed to have seen the bird. On the strength of their evidence field surveys were done, and in the early hours of January 13, 1986, near the Lankamalai Hills a single Jerdon's courser was spotted in the beam of a flashlight and captured.

Subsequent searches have usually been conducted in the hours of darkness, since the species appears to feed at night—a habit that could help explain its elusiveness. Sightings of birds at six further localities in three hill ranges of southern Andhra Pradesh revealed what is probably a single, small population.

INDIA

SRI LANKA

DATA PANEL

Jerdon's courser

Rhinoptilus bitorquatus

Family: Glareolidae

World population: Estimated at 50–250

Distribution: Eastern Ghats (mountain range) of states of Andhra Pradesh and extreme southern Madhya Pradesh in eastern India

Habitat: Rolling, rocky foothills with dense scrub forest and bushes (including thorny and nonthorny species), interspersed with open areas of bare ground

Size: Length: about 10.5 in (27 cm)

Form: Slender-bodied, smallish, ploverlike bird; shortish, yellow-based, black arched bill; longish, pale-yellowish legs. Plumage has complex pattern with distinctive pair of brown breast bands (the upper one much broader) separated by a white band; mainly blackish-brown crown and hind neck; broad, white eyestripes and broad, blackish-brown band behind each eye; orange-chestnut patch on white throat; upperparts mainly brown, apart from pattern of breast banding, underparts mainly white; in flight, brown wings with black primary flight feathers

that have white patch near tips; black tail with white base

Diet: Poorly known; feeds at night, probably on insects

Breeding: The only egg ever found was taken from a nest in 1917 but not identified until 2013 when its DNA was analysed

Related endangered species: Not a courser, but in same family: black-winged pratincole (*Glareola nordmanni*) NT

Status: IUCN CR

Habitat Destruction

It is likely that Jerdon's courser was never numerous. Its small, localized populations were possibly driven to the verge of extinction by overgrazing and disturbance in the special habitat it favors. The bird prefers scrubby forest (including dense thorn bushes) for sheltering from danger and patches of bare, open ground where it can find insect prey.

Today the courser's habitat is under greater threat than ever, being increasingly scarce and fragmented. After a dam was built in the region at Somasilla, the inhabitants of 57 villages were relocated to areas within the bird's range. The settlers depend on the surrounding landscape for fuel and grazing land for their livestock; such uses are likely to put increasing pressure on the remaining courser population. A further threat to the habitat comes from extensive quarrying operations. In addition, the increased disturbance by the villagers may directly affect the birds themselves.

Urgent Measures

In an effort to pull the little-known bird back from the brink of extinction, a wildlife sanctuary and national park were established in the region in response to the species' rediscovery. Concerted lobbying of the authorities by conservation groups has ensured that plans for a canal to pass through one of the protected areas were revised and that the canal was realigned. Already members of the local community have been employed to try to find more of the coursers.

Surveys to discover the bird's precise distribution, population size, and ecological needs in its presumed range are urgent if Jerdon's courser is to survive. Two reserves have been established in areas where it is thought to live: Sri Lankamaleswara and Sri Penusula. Two coursers were sighted in 2009, the first observations for several years. Camera traps have been placed in suitable locations to photograph the birds as they feed at night, but between 2010 and 2012 they had not photographed a single bird.

Jerdon's courser *was thought to be extinct. More needs to be known about the bird to help protect it, including its distribution and breeding habits.*

Spoon-billed Sandpiper

Eurynorhynchus pygmeus

Its small population and precise nesting requirements, and especially habitat disturbance at its migration and wintering sites, have made the future of the spoon-billed sandpiper uncertain.

The spoon-billed sandpiper has an extraordinary bill with an expanded diamond-shaped "spoon" tip. The bill is an adaptation to the bird's unusual feeding technique, in which it moves through shallow water, rapidly turning its head from side to side so that its bill sweeps the water's surface in semicircles. As with other sandpipers, the bill has touch-sensitive cells at its tip that can detect the movements of tiny invertebrates living in water or soft mud. The widened tip probably gives the bird a larger area of sensitivity to the vibrations caused by its prey and allows it to take in more with each snap.

Unlike many waders, which nest in a variety of coastal habitats, spoon-billed sandpipers have exacting requirements. They visit their breeding haunts in summer, a narrow band of coast around the Chukotski Peninsula in northeastern Siberia, and, farther south, along the isthmus (narrow strip of land) connecting to the Kamchatka Peninsula. Within their restricted breeding range they choose only sandy ridges with sparse vegetation along the shores of shallow coastal lagoons. They also prefer the inner parts of bays where certain river estuaries enter the sea, forming a complex patchwork of water channels and moss-covered shingle banks. Such specific requirements account for their patchy distribution within their overall range.

Winter Quarters

Every fall, spoon-billed sandpipers undergo a long and potentially hazardous journey to the coasts of subtropical and tropical South and Southeast Asia for the winter. The females leave first; their mates

DATA PANEL

Spoon-billed sandpiper

Eurynorhynchus pygmeus

Family: Scolopacidae

World population: 120–200 pairs (2010 estimate)

Distribution: Breeds in northeastern Siberia, Russia; winters in South and Southeast Asia

Habitat: Nests on coasts with sandy ridges near marshes and lakes; winters on coasts, especially by deltas and lagoons

Size: Length: 5.5–6.3 in (14–16 cm). Weight: male about 1 oz (29.5 g); female about 1.3 oz (35 g)

Form: Small, plump-bodied bird with distinctive spatula-shaped bill. In breeding plumage has dark-streaked, reddish-brown head, neck, and breast; blackish back; buff and pale-reddish fringes to wing feathers; white belly; black legs and bill. In nonbreeding plumage has pale-grayish upperparts, prominent white stripe above eyes, and all-white underparts. Juveniles similar to winter adults, but browner

Diet: Insects and their larvae, both land-dwelling and aquatic, including beetles, flies, and small wasps; other aquatic invertebrates such as crustaceans; also small seeds

Breeding: In June and July scrapes out a hollow, sometimes lined with leaves, among low vegetation; 4 brown-blotched buff eggs are laid; incubation 18–20 days; fledging period 15–20 days. Male matures at 2 years, female probably at 1 year

Related endangered species: Nine other species of sandpipers and relatives, including eskimo curlew (*Numenius borealis*) CR; slender-billed curlew (*N. tenuirostris*) CR; spotted greenshank (*Tringa guttifer*) EN, and Tuamotu sandpiper (*Prosobonia cancellata*) EN

Status: IUCN CR

tend their brood of chicks from when they are five or six days old for a further 10 to15 days. The males then leave the breeding area, and eventually, so do the young; some young linger on in the nesting grounds until mid-October. In their winter quarters the sandpipers prefer deltas and lagoons with mud banks, sand banks, or small islands.

Most spoon-billed sandpipers spend the winter on the coast of Myanmar and Bangladesh, which they reach after a migration of 5,000 miles (8,000 km). They rest and feed on the intertidal zone at locations along the route in China, Vietnam, and Thailand. The most important of these stopover sites was not discovered until 2013, when 140 birds were located on the coast north of Shanghai, China. In Myanmar, Bangladesh, and parts of China impoverished fishers catch shorebirds—including 'spoonies'—in nets. This explains some of the decline in the birds' numbers, and the reclamation of large sections of the coast of China for industry has also denied them places to feed. In comparison, they face few problems on their Siberian breeding grounds.

The spoon-billed sandpiper *has a bill with a broad and flattened tip.*

In the 1970s there were 2,000–2,800 pairs on the breeding grounds, but this number declined to fewer than 1,000 pairs in 2000, 402–572 pairs in 2003, and 120–200 pairs in 2010. To counter this catastrophic decline, drastic action was needed.

Drastic Action

Conservationists now work with coastal communities in Myanmar and Bangladesh to persuade them not to hunt the sandpipers. Pressure has been placed on governments along the migration flyway to protect the birds' stopover sites. In 2012 and 2013 eggs were taken from some sandpiper nests and incubated. The hatched chicks were hand-reared, while the adults laid a second clutch of eggs to replace those that had been taken from them. A total of 25 hand-reared birds were then allowed to join the other young birds and migrate south with them in the fall. It is known that at least two of them did so successfully. One major disaster could wipe out such a tiny population, so as a precautionary measure some eggs were taken to the UK, where they were incubated, hatched, and hand-reared. If all else fails, the future of the spoon-billed sandpiper could rest with these captive birds.

Categories of Threat

The status categories that appear in the data panel for each species throughout this book are based on those published by the International Union for the Conservation of Nature (IUCN). They provide a useful guide to the current status of the species in the wild, and governments throughout the world use them when assessing conservation priorities and in policy making. However, they do not provide automatic legal protection for the species.

Animals are placed in the appropriate category after scientific research. More species are being added all the time, and animals can be moved from one category to another as their circumstances change.

Extinct (EX)

A group of animals is classified as EX when there is no reasonable doubt that the last individual has died.

Extinct in the Wild (EW)

Animals in this category are known to survive only in captivity or as a population established artificially by introduction somewhere well outside its former range. A species is categorized as EW when exhaustive surveys throughout the areas where it used to occur consistently fail to record a single individual. It is important that such searches be carried out over all of the available habitat and during a season or time of day when the animals should be present.

Critically Endangered (CR)

The category CR includes animals facing an extremely high risk of extinction in the wild in the immediate future. It includes any of the following:

• Any species with fewer than 50 individuals, even if the population is stable.
• Any species with fewer than 250 individuals if the population is declining, badly fragmented, or all in one vulnerable group.
• Animals from larger populations that have declined by 80 percent within 10 years (or are predicted to do so) or three generations, whichever is the longer.

The IUCN categories
of threat. The system displayed has operated for new and reviewed assessments since January 2001.

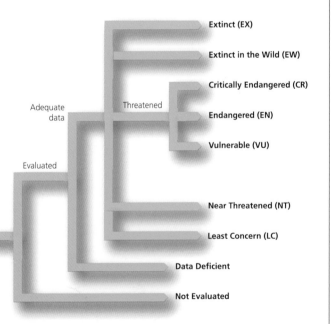

- Extinct (EX)
- Extinct in the Wild (EW)
- Critically Endangered (CR)
- Endangered (EN)
- Vulnerable (VU)
- Near Threatened (NT)
- Least Concern (LC)
- Data Deficient
- Not Evaluated

Adequate data

Threatened

Evaluated

• Species living in a very small area—defined as under 39 square miles (100 sq. km).

Endangered (EN)

A species is EN when it is not CR but is nevertheless facing a very high risk of extinction in the wild in the near future. It includes any of the following:

• A species with fewer than 250 individuals remaining, even if the population is stable.

• Any species with fewer than 2,500 individuals if the population is declining, badly fragmented, or all in one vulnerable subpopulation.

• A species whose population is known or expected to decline by 50 percent within 10 years or three generations, whichever is the longer.

• A species whose range is under 1,900 square miles (5,000 sq. km), and whose range, numbers, or population levels are declining, fragmented, or fluctuating wildly.

• Species for which there is a more than 20 percent likelihood of extinction in the next 20 years or five generations, whichever is the longer.

Vulnerable (VU)

A species is VU when it is not CR or EN but is facing a high risk of extinction in the wild in the medium-term future. It includes any of the following:

• A species with fewer than 1,000 mature individuals remaining, even if the population is stable.

• Any species with fewer than 10,000 individuals if the population is declining, badly fragmented, or all in one vulnerable subpopulation.

The population *of the snow leopard (left) is still declining as a result of habitat loss, a decline in the animals it hunts, poaching, and persecution. It is considered to be Endangered, but if its numbers fall further this magnificent cat could be reclassified as Critically Endangered.*

• A species whose population is known, believed, or expected to decline by 20 percent within 10 years or three generations, whichever is the longer.

• A species whose range is less than 7,700 square miles (20,000 sq. km), and whose range, numbers, or population structure are declining, fragmented, or fluctuating wildly.

• Species for which there is a more than 10 percent likelihood of extinction in the next 100 years.

Near Threatened/Least Concern (since 2001)

In January 2001 the classification of lower-risk species was changed. Near Threatened (NT) and Least Concern (LC) were introduced as separate categories. They replaced the previous Lower Risk (LR) category with its subdivisions of Conservation Dependent (LRcd), Near Threatened (LRnt), and Least Concern (LRlc). From January 2001 all new assessments and reassessments must adopt NT or LC if relevant. But the older categories still apply to some animals until they are reassessed.

• Near Threatened (NT)
Animals that do not qualify for CR, EN, or VU categories now but are close to qualifying or are likely to qualify for a threatened category in the future.

• Least Concern (LC)
Animals that have been evaluated and do not qualify for CR, EN, VU, or NT categories.

Lower Risk (before 2001)

• Conservation Dependent (LRcd)
Animals whose survival depends on an existing conservation program.

• Near Threatened (LRnt)
Animals for which there is no conservation program but that are close to qualifying for VU category.

• Least Concern (LRlc)
Species that are not conservation dependent or near threatened.

The Nilgiri tahr *lives in a relatively small mountainous area of southern India and has long been hunted for its meat, although it is now protected. With a small and declining population, its status is Endangered.*

Data Deficient (DD)

A species or population is DD when there is not enough information on abundance and distribution to assess the risk of extinction. In some cases, when the species is thought to live only in a small area, or a considerable period of time has passed since the species was last recorded, it may be placed in a threatened category as a precaution.

Not Evaluated (NE)

Such animals have not yet been assessed.

Note: a colored panel in each entry in this book indicates the current level of threat to the species. The two new categories (NT and LC) include the earlier Lower Risk categories (LRcd and LRnt); the old LRlc is included along with Data Deficient (DD) and Not Evaluated (NE) under "Other," abbreviated to "O."

CITES *lists animals in the major groups in three appendices, depending on the level of threat posed by international trade.*

	Appendix I	Appendix II	Appendix III
Mammals	297 species 23 subspecies 2 populations	492 species 5 subspecies 5 populations	44 species 10 subspecies
Birds	156 species 11 subspecies 2 populations	1,275 species 2 subspecies	24 species
Reptiles	76 species 5 subspecies 1 population	582 species 6 populations	56 species
Amphibians	17 species	113 species	1 species
Fish	15 species	81 species	
Invertebrates	64 species 5 subspecies	2,142 species 1 subspecies	17 species 3 subspecies

CITES APPENDICES

Appendix I lists the most endangered of traded species, namely those that are threatened with extinction and will be harmed by continued trade. These species are usually protected in their native countries and can only be imported or exported with a special permit. Permits are required to cover the whole transaction—both exporter and importer must prove that there is a compelling scientific justification for moving the animal from one country to another. This includes transferring animals between zoos for breeding purposes. Permits are only issued when it can be proved that the animal was legally acquired and that the remaining population will not be harmed by taking it from its natural habitat.

Appendix II includes species not currently threatened with extinction but could easily become so if trade is not carefully controlled. Some common animals are listed here if they resemble endangered species so closely that criminals could try to sell the rare species pretending they were a similar common one. Permits are required to export such animals, with requirements similar to those Appendix I species.

Appendix III species are those that are at risk or protected in at least one country. Other nations may be allowed to trade in animals or products, but they may need to prove that they come from safe populations.

CITES designations are not always the same for every country. In some cases individual countries can apply for special permission to trade in a listed species. For example, they might have a safe population of an animal that is very rare elsewhere. Some African countries periodically apply for permission to export large quantities of elephant tusks that have been in storage for years, or that are the product of a legal cull of elephants. This is controversial because it creates an opportunity for criminals to dispose of black market ivory by passing it off as coming from one of those countries where elephant products are allowed to be exported. The African elephant, for example, is listed as CITES I, II, and III, depending on the country location of the different populations.

Organizations

The human race is undoubtedly nature's worst enemy, but we can also help limit the damage caused by the rapid increase in our numbers and activities. There have always been people eager to protect the world's beautiful places and to preserve its most special animals, but it is only quite recently that the conservation message has begun to have a real effect on everyday life, government policy, industry, and agriculture.

Early conservationists were concerned with preserving nature for the benefit of people. They acted with an instinctive sense of what was good for nature and people, arguing for the preservation of wilderness and animals in the same way as others argued for the conservation of historic buildings or gardens. The study of ecology and environmental science did not really take off until the mid-20th century, and it took a long time for the true scale of our effect on the natural world to become apparent. Today the conservation of wildlife is based on far greater scientific understanding, but the situation has become much more complex and urgent in the face of human development.

By the mid-20th century extinction was becoming an immediate threat. Animals such as the passenger pigeon, quagga, and thylacine had disappeared despite last-minute attempts to save them. More and more species were discovered to be at risk, and species-focused conservation groups began to appear. In the early days there was little that any of these organizations could do but campaign against direct killing. Later they became a kind of conservation emergency service—rushing to the aid of seriously threatened animals in an attempt to save the species. But as time went on, broader environmental issues began to receive the urgent attention they needed. Research showed time and time again that saving species almost always comes down to addressing the problem of habitat loss. The world is short of space, and ensuring that there is enough for all the species is very difficult.

Conservation is not just about animals and plants, nor even the protection of whole ecological systems. Conservation issues are so broad that they touch almost every aspect of our lives, and successful measures often depend on the expertise of biologists, ecologists, economists, diplomats, lawyers, social scientists, and businesspeople. Conservation is all about cooperation and teamwork. Often it is also about helping people benefit from taking care of their wildlife. The organizations involved vary from small groups of a few dozen enthusiasts in local communities to vast, multinational operations.

With so much activity based in different countries, it is important to have a worldwide overview—some way of coordinating what goes on in different parts of the planet. That is the role of the International Union for the Conservation of Nature (IUCN), also referred to as the World Conservation Union. It began life as the International Union for the Preservation of Nature in 1948, becoming the IUCN in 1956. It is relatively new compared to the Sierra Club, Flora and Fauna International, and the Royal Society for the Protection of Birds. It was remarkable in that its founder members included governments, government agencies, and nongovernmental organizations. In the years following the appalling destruction of World War II, the IUCN was born out of a desire to draw a line under the horrors of the past and to act together to safeguard the future.

The mission of the IUCN is to influence, encourage, and assist societies throughout the world to conserve the diversity of nature and natural systems. It seeks to ensure that the use of natural resources is fair and ecologically sustainable. Based in Switzerland, the IUCN

Mai Po nature reserve *in Hong Kong is a very important refuge for shorebirds and other water birds, including spoon-billed sandpipers and black-faced spoonbills. It is managed by the World Wide Fund for Nature.*

has over 1,000 permanent staff and the help of 11,000 volunteer experts from about 180 countries. The work of the IUCN is split into six commissions, which deal with protected areas, policy-making, ecosystem management, education, environmental law, and species survival. The Species Survival Commission (SSC) has almost 7,000 members, all experts in the study of plants and animals. Within the SSC there are Specialist Groups concerned with the conservation of different types of animals, from cats to flamingos, deer, ducks, bats, and crocodiles. Some particularly well-studied animals, such as the African elephant and the polar bear, have their own specialist groups.

Perhaps the best-known role of the IUCN SSC is in the production of the Red Data Books, or Red List. First published in 1966, the books were designed to

be easily updated, with details of each species on a different page that could be removed and replaced as new information came to light.

By 2013 the Red List includes information on about 53,000 types of animal, of which more than 11,000 are threatened with extinction. Gathering this amount of information together is a huge task, but it provides an invaluable conservation resource. The Red List is continually updated and is now available online. The Red List is the basis for the categories of threat used in this book.

CITES is the Convention on International Trade in Endangered Species of Wild Fauna and Flora (also known as the Washington Convention, since it first came into force after an international meeting in Washington D.C. in 1973). Currently 175 nations have agreed to implement the CITES regulations. Exceptions to the convention include Iraq and North Korea, which, for the time being at least, have few trading links with the rest of the world. Trading in animals and their body parts has been a major factor in the decline of some of the world's rarest species. The IUCN categories draw attention to the status of rare species, but they do not confer any legal protection. That is done through national laws.

Conventions serve as international laws. In the case of CITES, lists (called appendices) are agreed on internationally and reviewed every few years. The appendices list the species that are threatened by international trade. Animals are assigned to Appendix I when all trade is forbidden. Any specimens of these species, alive or dead (or skins, feathers, etc.), will be confiscated by customs at international borders, seaports, or airports. Appendix II species can be traded internationally, but only under strict controls. Wildlife trade is often valuable in the rural economy, and this raises difficult questions about the relative importance of animals and people. Nevertheless, traders who ignore CITES rules risk heavy fines or imprisonment. Some rare species—even those with the highest IUCN categories (many bats and frogs, for example)—may have no CITES protection simply because they have no commercial value. Trade is then not really a threat.

WILDLIFE CONSERVATION ORGANIZATIONS

BirdLife International
BirdLife International is a partnership of 60 organizations working in more than 100 countries. Most partners are national nongovernmental conservation groups. Others include large bird charities. By working within BirdLife International, even small organizations can be effective globally as well as on a local scale.
www.birdlife.org

Conservation International (CI)
Founded in 1987, Conservation International works closely with the IUCN and has a similar multinational approach.
www.conservation.org

Durrell Wildlife Conservation Trust (DWCT)
The Durrell Wildlife Conservation Trust was founded by the British naturalist and author Gerald Durrell in 1963. The trust is based at Durrell's zoo on Jersey in the Channel Islands. Jersey Zoo and the DWCT were instrumental in saving many species from extinction, including the pink pigeon, Mauritius kestrel, Waldrapp ibis, St. Lucia parrot, and Telfair's skink.
www.durrell.org

Fauna & Flora International (FFI)
Founded in 1903, this organization has had various name changes. It began life as a society for protecting large mammals, but has broadened its scope. It was involved in saving the Arabian oryx from extinction.
www.fauna-flora.org

National Audubon Society
John James Audubon was an American naturalist and wildlife artist who died in 1851, 35 years before the society that bears his name was founded. The first Audubon Society was established by George Bird Grinnell in protest against the appalling overkill of birds for meat, feathers, and sport. By the end of the 19th century there were Audubon Societies in 15 states, and they later became part of the National Audubon Society, which funds scientific research programs, publishes magazines and journals, manages wildlife sanctuaries, and advises state and federal governments on conservation.
www.audubon.org

The Sierra Club
The Sierra Club was started in 1892 by John Muir. It was through Muir's efforts that the first national parks, including Yosemite, Sequoia, and Mount Rainier, were established. The Sierra Club remains dedicated to the preservation of wild places for the benefit of wildlife and people.
www.sierraclub.org

World Wide Fund for Nature (WWF)
The World Wide Fund for Nature, formerly the World Wildlife Fund, was born in 1961. It was a joint venture between the IUCN, several existing conservation organizations, and a number of successful businesspeople. WWF was big, well funded, and high profile from the beginning. Its familiar giant panda emblem is instantly recognizable.
www.wwf.org

More Endangered Animals

This is the second series of Facts at Your Fingertips: Endangered Animals. Many other endangered animals were included in the first series, which was broken down by animal class, as follows:

BIRDS
Northern Brown Kiwi
Galápagos Penguin
Bermuda Petrel
Andean Flamingo
Northern Bald Ibis
White-headed Duck
Nene
Philippine Eagle
Spanish Imperial Eagle
Red Kite
California Condor
Mauritius Kestrel
Whooping Crane
Takahe
Kakapo
Hyacinth Macaw
Pink Pigeon
Spotted Owl
Bee Hummingbird
Regent Honeyeater
Blue Bird of Paradise
Raso Lark
Gouldian Finch

FISH
Coelacanth
Great White Shark
Common Sturgeon
Danube Salmon
Lake Victoria Haplochromine Cichlids
Dragon Fish
Silver Shark
Whale Shark
Northern Bluefin Tuna
Masked Angelfish
Big Scale Archerfish
Bandula Barb
Mekong Giant Catfish
Alabama Cavefish
Blind Cave Characin
Atlantic Cod
Mountain Blackside Dace
Lesser Spiny Eel
Australian Lungfish
Paddlefish
Ornate Paradisefish
Knysna Seahorse
Spring Pygmy Sunfish

INVERTEBRATES
Broad Sea Fan
Giant Gippsland Earthworm
Edible Sea-Urchin
Velvet Worms
Southern Damselfly
Orange-spotted Emerald
Red-kneed Tarantula
Kauai Cave Wolf Spider
Great Raft Spider
European Red Wood Ant
Hermit Beetle
Blue Ground Beetle
Birdwing Butterfly
Apollo Butterfly
Avalon Hairstreak Butterfly
Hermes Copper Butterfly
Giant Clam
California Bay Pea Crab
Horseshoe Crab
Cushion Star
Freshwater Mussel
Starlet Sea Anemone
Partula Snails

MAMMALS OF THE NORTHERN HEMISPHERE
Asiatic Lion
Tiger
Clouded Leopard
Iberian Lynx
Florida Panther
Wildcat
Gray Wolf
Swift Fox
Polar Bear
Giant Panda
European Mink
Pine Marten
Black-footed Ferret
Wolverine
Sea Otter
Steller's Sea Lion
Mediterranean Monk Seal
Florida Manatee
Przewalski's Wild Horse
American Bison
Arabian Oryx
Wild Yak
Ryukyu Flying Fox

MAMMALS OF THE SOUTHERN HEMISPHERE
Cheetah
Leopard
Jaguar
Spectacled Bear
Giant Otter
Amazon River Dolphin
Sperm Whale
Blue Whale
Humpback Whale
Proboscis Monkey
Chimpanzee
Mountain Gorilla
Orang-Utan
Ruffed Lemur
African Elephant
Black Rhinoceros
Giant Otter Shrew
Mulgara
Kangaroo Island Dunnart
Marsupial Mole
Koala
Long-beaked Echidna
Platypus

REPTILES AND AMPHIBIANS
Blunt-nosed Leopard Lizard
Pygmy Blue-tongued Skink
Komodo Dragon
Hawksbill Turtle
Yellow-blotched Sawback Map Turtle
Galápagos Giant Tortoise
Jamaican Boa
Woma Python
Milos Viper
Chinese Alligator
American Crocodile
Gharial
Gila Monster
Japanese Giant Salamander
Olm
Mallorcan Midwife Toad
Golden Toad
Western Toad
Golden Mantella
Tomato Frog
Gastric-brooding Frog

GLOSSARY

adaptation Features of an animal that adjust it to its environment; may be produced by evolution—e.g. camouflage coloration

adaptive radiation Where a group of closely related animals (e.g. members of a family) have evolved differences from each other so that they can survive in different niches

adult A fully grown, sexually mature animal; a bird in its final plumage

anterior The front part of an animal

arboreal Living in trees

bill The jaws of a bird, consisting of two bony mandibles, upper and lower, and their horny sheaths

biodiversity The variety of species and the variation within them

biome A major world landscape characterized by having similar plants and animals living in it, e.g. desert, rain forest, forest

breeding season The entire cycle of reproductive activity, from courtship, pair formation (and often establishment of territory) through nesting to independence of young

brood The young hatching from a single clutch of eggs

browsing Feeding on leaves of trees and shrubs

canine tooth A sharp stabbing tooth usually longer than the rest

carnivore An animal that eats other animals

carrion Rotting flesh of dead animals

cloaca Cavity in the pelvic region into which the alimentary canal, genital, and urinary ducts open

deforestation The process of cutting down and removing trees for timber or to create open space for growing crops, grazing animals, etc.

desert Area of low rainfall, typically with sparse scrub or grassland vegetation or lacking it altogether

diurnal Active during the day

DNA (deoxyribonucleic acid) The substance that makes up the main part of the chromosomes of all living things; contains the genetic code that is handed down from generation to generation

dormancy A state in which—as a result of hormone action—growth is suspended and metabolic activity is reduced to a minimum

dorsal Relating to the back or spinal part of the body; usually the upper surface

ecology The study of plants and animals in relation to one another and to their surroundings

ecosystem A whole system in which plants, animals, and their environment interact

endemic Found only in one geographical area, nowhere else

eutrophication An increase in the nutrient chemicals (nitrate, phosphate, etc.) in water, sometimes occurring naturally and sometimes caused by human activities, e.g. by the release of sewage or agricultural fertilizers

extinction Process of dying out at the end of which the very last individual dies, and the species is lost forever

feral Domestic animals that have gone wild and live independently of people

gene The basic unit of heredity, enabling one generation to pass on characteristics to its offspring

gestation The period of pregnancy in mammals, between fertilization of the egg and birth of the baby

herbivore An animal that eats plants (grazers and browsers are herbivores)

hibernation Becoming inactive in winter, with lowered body temperature to save energy. Hibernation takes place in a special nest or den called a hibernaculum

homeotherm An animal that can maintain a high and constant body temperature by means of internal processes; also called "warm-blooded"

inbreeding Breeding among closely related animals (e.g. cousins), leading to weakened genetic composition and reduced survival rates

incubation The act of keeping eggs warm for the period from laying the eggs to hatching

insectivore Animal that feeds on insects. Also used as a group name for hedgehogs, shrews, moles, etc.

keratin Tough, fibrous material that forms hair, feathers, nails, and protective plates on the skin of vertebrate animals

mammal Any animal of the class Mammalia—a warm-blooded vertebrate having mammary glands in the female that produce milk with which it nurses its young. The class includes bats, primates, rodents, and whales

metabolic rate The rate at which chemical activities occur within animals, including the exchange of gasses in respiration and the liberation of energy from food

metamorphosis The transformation of a larva into an adult

migration Movement from one place to another and back again; usually seasonal

molt The process in which some mammals regularly shed their fur, birds replace their feathers, and reptiles shed their skin

omnivore An animal that eats a wide range of both animal and vegetable food

parasite An animal or plant that lives on or within the body of another (the host) from which it obtains nourishment. The host is often harmed by the association

pheromone Scent produced by animals to enable others to find and recognize them

placenta The structure that links an embryo to its mother during pregnancy, allowing exchange of chemicals between them

plumage The covering of feathers on a bird's body

posterior The hind end or behind another structure

predator An animal that kills live prey

quadruped Any animal that walks on four legs

raptor Bird with hooked bill and strong feet with sharp claws (talons) for seizing, killing, and dealing with prey; also known as birds of prey

species A group of animals that look similar and can breed with each other to produce fertile offspring

steppe Open grassland in parts of the world where the climate is too harsh for trees to grow

tundra Open grassy or shrub-covered lands of the far north

understory The layer of shrubs, herbs, and small trees found beneath the forest canopy

vertebrate Animal with a backbone (e.g. fish, mammal, reptile), usually with skeleton made of bones, but sometimes softer cartilage

wintering ground The area where a migrant spends time outside the breeding season

FURTHER RESEARCH

Books

Mammals

Angel, H., *Pandas*, Voyageur Press, Minneapolis, U.S., 1998

Gurung, K., and Singh, R., *Field Guide to the Mammals of the Indian Subcontinent,* Princeton University Press, Princeton, U.S., 2009

Macdonald, David, ed., *The New Encyclopedia of Mammals,* Oxford University Press, Oxford, U.K., 2009

Menon, V., *Mammals of India*, Princeton University Press, Princeton, U.S., 2009

Scherer, G., and Fletcher, M., *The Snow Leopard: Help Save Endangered Species,* Enslow, New York, U.S., 2007

Wilson, Don E., Mittermeier, Russell A., *Handbook of Mammals of the World Vol 1,* Lynx Edicions, Barcelona, Spain, 2009

Birds

Attenborough, David, *The Life of Birds,* BBC Books, London, U.K., 1998

Ayé, R., Schweizer, M., and Roth, T., *Birds of Central Asia*, Christopher Helm, London, U.K., 2012

BirdLife International, *State of the World's Birds: Indicators for our Changing World*, BirdLife International, Cambridge, U.K., 2008

del Hoyo, J., Elliott, A., and Sargatal, J., eds, *Handbook of Birds of the World Vols 1 to 15,* Lynx Edicions, Barcelona, Spain, 1992–2013

Harris, Tim, *Migration Hotspots of the World*, Bloomsbury/RSPB, London, U.K., 2013

Inskipp, C., Grimmett, R., and Inskipp, T., *Birds of the Indian Subcontinent*, Christopher Helm, London, U.K., 2012

Stattersfield, A., Crosby, M., Long, A., and Wege, D., eds, *Endemic Bird Areas of the World: Priorities for Biodiversity Conservation,* BirdLife International, Cambridge, U.K., 1998

General

Allaby, Michael, *A Dictionary of Ecology*, Oxford University Press, New York, U.S., 2010

Douglas, Dougal, and others, *Atlas of Life on Earth*, Barnes & Noble, New York, U.S., 2001

Websites

www.birdlife.org The site of BirdLife International, highlighting projects to protect the populations of endangered species

www.cites.org CITES and IUCN listings. Search for animals by order, family, genus, species, or common name. Location by country and explanation of reasons for listings

www.darwinfoundation.org Charles Darwin Research Center

www.edgeofexistence.com Highlights and conserves one-of-a-kind species that are on the verge of extinction

www.endangeredspecie.com Information, links, books, and publications about rare and endangered species. Also includes information about conservation efforts and organizations

eol.org/pages/326452/overview Lots of information about black crested gibbons from Encyclopedia of Life

www.fauna-flora.org Information about animals and plants around the world on the site of the Flora and Fauna Conservation Society

www.forests.org Includes answers to queries about forest conservation

www.iucn.org Details of species, IUCN listings, and IUCN publications. Link to online Red List of threatened species at: *www.iucnredlist.org*

www.nationalgeographic.co.uk/animals/mammals/sloth-bear Photos and information about the sloth bear and its lifestyle

www.panda.org World Wide Fund for Nature (WWF). Newsroom, press releases, government reports, campaigns. Themed photogallery

www.wcs.org Wildlife Conservation Society site. Information on projects to help endangered animals in every continent.

www.wildcattle.org A site aiming to increase knowledge about wild cattle (including the gaur of South Asia) worldwide, and assist with their conservation

worldwildlife.org/species/asian-elephant WWF's online pages on the Asian elephant, including information on its lifestyle, where it lives, and measures to help it survive

worldwildlife.org/species/greater-one-horned-rhino WWF's online pages on the one-horned, or great Indian, rhinoceros, including facts about its lifestyle and measures to help its conservation

worldwildlife.org/species/red-panda WWF's online pages on the red, or lesser, panda, including facts about its lifestyle and forest habitat and the measures planned to help its conservation

worldwildlife.org/species/snow-leopard WWF's online pages on the snow leopard, its lifestyle, threats to its population, and conservation measures to help it survive

INDEX

Page numbers in **bold** indicate
main references to the animals.